Understanding the Stranger

Building bridges community handbook

Practical lessons for practitioners, policymakers and funders aiming to combat asylum-related community tension between host communities and refugees and asylum seekers

Neil Amas and Beth Crosland
INFORMATION CENTRE ABOUT ASYLUM AND REFUGEES

Published by
Calouste Gulbenkian Foundation
United Kingdom Branch
98 Portland Place
London W1B 1ET
Tel: 020 7908 7604
E-mail: info@gulbenkian.org.uk
Website: www.gulbenkian.org.uk

All rights reserved; unauthorised reproduction of any part of this work in any medium is strictly prohibited.

© 2006 Calouste Gulbenkian Foundation

The right of Neil Amas and Beth Crosland to be identified as the authors of this work has been asserted in accordance with the Copyright, Designs and Patents Act 1988.

The views expressed in this book are those of the authors, not necessarily those of the Calouste Gulbenkian Foundation.

ISBN 1 903080 06 1
ISBN (13) 9781 903080 06 1

British Library Cataloguing-in-Publication Data
A catalogue record for this book is available from the British Library

Edited by Christopher McDowell
Designed by Bananadesign www.bananadesign.co.uk
Printed by Stephen Austin Printers, SG13 7LU

Distributed by Central Books Ltd, 99 Wallis Road, London E9 5LN
Tel: 0845 458 9911, Fax: 0845 458 9912
E-mail: orders@centralbooks.com
Website: www.centralbooks.com

Contents

Acknowledgements 4

Preface 5

Foreword 6

Introduction 7

Methodology 13

Case Studies

COMMUNITY DEVELOPMENT
1. Leicester North West Community Forum 15
2. Refugee Accommodate Project, Canopy Housing 18

DEVELOPING RESPONSIVE PUBLIC SERVICES
3. Camden Scrutiny Panel, Camden Council 22
4. Community Outreach Team and the New Communities Team, Southampton City Council 25
5. Regional Community Cohesion Project, North West Asylum Seekers Consortium 28
6. Walsall Wardens Scheme 31
7. Welcome to Your Library, London Libraries Development Agency 34

INCREASING UNDERSTANDING
8. Cooking Project, Centrepoint 37
9. Enfield Asylum Seekers Scrutiny Commission Panel, Enfield Council 40
10. Refugee Awareness Project, Refugee Action 43

LOCAL INTEGRATION
11. Football Project, Asylum Seekers and Refugees of Kingston-upon-Hull 47
12. Derwent Zambezi Association 50
13. Derwent Refugee Community Development Support Project, Refugee Action 54
14. Greater Pollock Settlement and Integration Network 57
15. Swansea Bay Asylum Seekers Support Group 62
16. Victoria Estate Action Group 65

PERSONAL DEVELOPMENT
17. The Bridges Project 68
18. Learning to Advise, Stoke Citizens Advice Bureau 71
19. Stress Leaflet Project, Mothertongue 74
20. Shared Road, Prince's Trust 76
21. Skye and Falinge Girls' Group, Greater Manchester Police 79

Summary 82

Concluding Remarks 86

Bibliography 87

Acknowledgements

ICAR is very grateful for the advice and guidance received from the following members of the Project Advisory Group:

Andrew Fleming, Home Office
Claire Griffin, Safe Communities, Commission for Racial Equality
Miranda Lewis, Institute for Public Policy Research
Mark Lyall, Association of Chief Police Officers
Richard McKeever, Community Links
Kirsteen Tait, Independent Consultant

The researchers would also like to express their gratitude to all those who agreed to be interviewed and for their valuable contributions, in particular:

Maggie Lennon, Bridges Project
George Binette and Vickie Skade, Camden Council
Tony Pascoe, Gavin Barker, Abdul Mohammed, Community Outreach Team and the New Communities Team, Southampton City Council
Jennie Blake, Cooking Project, Centrepoint
Gail Pringle, Derwent Refugee Community Development Support Project, Refugee Action
Emilio Tavares, Derwent Zambezi Association
Mike Ahuja, Enfield Asylum Seekers Scrutiny Commission Panel, Enfield Council
Lynne Colley, Football Project, Asylum Seekers and Refugees of Kingston-upon-Hull
Linda McGlynn, George Daly and Beltus Etchu, Greater Pollock Settlement and Integration Network
Jude Hawes, Jutta Möhrke, Semere Yohannes, Said M. Muruts and Faiza Shab, Learning to Advise, Stoke Citizens Advice Bureau
Jean-Didier Mualaba, Leicester North West Community Forum
Mark Stevens, Refugee Accommodate Project, Canopy Housing
Esme Peach, Refugee Awareness Project, Refugee Action
Emma Read, Regional Community Cohesion Project, North West Asylum Seekers Consortium
Ken Imrie, Shared Road, Prince's Trust
Tracey Lowe, Skye and Falinge Girls' Group, Greater Manchester Police
Beverley Costa, Stress Leaflet Project, Mothertongue
Tom Cheesman, Swansea Bay Asylum Seekers Support Group
Vera Walker, Victoria Estate Action Group
Natalie Jones, Bashir Ahmed, Yasmeen Nawaz and Abdul Kalam, Walsall Wardens Scheme
Helen Carpenter, Welcome to Your Library, London Libraries Development Agency

Preface

The Gulbenkian Foundation commissioned *Understanding the Stranger* from ICAR a year ago. It seemed to us useful that ICAR's expert knowledge of the difficulties faced by refugees and asylum seekers in coming to live in the UK should be disseminated more widely in order that society might deal effectively with their problems and also with the concerns of the host communities. We hope the narrative and case studies that follow will help those seeking a more positive approach to making strangers into friends and neighbours, learning from them and valuing their skills.

Understanding the Stranger is published at a time of worldwide debate on migratory movements. In 2003 the United Nations set up a Global Commission on International Migration, which released a 90-page report of findings and recommendations last year. In September 2006 its General Assembly will hold a High-level Dialogue on the issue. The book also complements the Gulbenkian's Forum on Immigration, a year-long programme of conferences, workshops, exhibitions and events being held by the Foundation in Lisbon until March 2007; and is part of the ongoing interest the UK Branch of the Foundation has been taking in this area.

We hope it will offer a real contribution to the debate and to understanding the stranger.

Paula Ridley
Director
Calouste Gulbenkian Foundation (UK Branch)

Foreword

Understanding the Stranger: Building bridges community handbook showcases and examines 21 projects from across the UK that aim to mediate tension and build bridges between local host communities and asylum seekers and refugees. The projects included are drawn from both the statutory and non-statutory sectors and include small-scale grassroots initiatives in urban settings.

The main purpose of the Handbook is to generate new thinking and ideas about practical initiatives that might contribute positively to local integration, community and personal development, increasing understanding and improving public services. Specifically, the publication draws on the experience of recent projects in order to offer guidance and contacts for individuals and organisations working at a local level. It aims also to transfer knowledge by ensuring that lessons learnt in one city, town or neighbourhood are readily available to others. The Handbook will be relevant for local authority staff, community-level strategic partnerships, neighbourhood wardens, tenants associations, Refugee Community Organisations (RCOs), voluntary, faith and other community organisations, sports and social clubs. But it will also be relevant for social entrepreneurs and members of the public and asylum and refugee communities who are considering schemes in their own areas. And the messages of the Handbook will be useful for policymakers and funders when deciding on strategy, what type of work to support and the evaluation of programmes and projects.

With the diversity of initiatives that it contains, the Handbook is appropriate for a broad range of socio-economic and demographic urban contexts in the UK. These include areas that are distinctly multicultural and those that are not. It is appropriate also for those parts of the UK that have relatively little experience of managing the arrival of asylum seekers and refugees, for small- and large-scale initiatives and for the voluntary and statutory sectors. Though all of the projects featured in the Handbook sought to address community-relations issues, for some there was an explicit aim to improve relations between the new and established communities whilst for others this was more implicit in an overall approach.

The Introduction provides a working definition of 'building bridges' and a discussion of current policy and academic thinking. A brief description of the research design is followed by a presentation of the case studies. The final section of the Handbook pulls together lessons learned and suggests ways ahead.

Introduction

It takes a leap of the imagination to picture the Zambezi River in southern Africa flowing into the River Derwent in Derbyshire. At the point of convergence, where a new bridge spans the two rivers, people from each side cross backwards and forwards, meeting, trading, exchanging ideas and over time adjusting to one another; each population subtly changing the nature of the other.

This is the inspiration for the work of the Derwent Zambezi Association community organisation in Derby, featured later in this Handbook. It also serves to illustrate the subtitle of *Understanding the Stranger: Building bridges community handbook*.

In the social rather than the construction world, 'building bridges' is generally understood to mean initiatives that aim 'to create a means of communication or understanding between people or a means of reconciling their differences'. The concept of 'bridging' in recent academic thinking refers to the relationships and links across social groups, first developed by American academic Robert Puttman following his fieldwork in Italy. Puttman popularised the notion of 'social capital' – the networks of trust that bind people, organisations and communities together: where 'bonding' describes relationships within a community, 'bridging' denotes connections across social groups, and 'linking' refers to networks between communities, agencies and institutions.

In this publication, 'building bridges' generally refers to local-level initiatives that attempt to bring together newly arrived refugees and asylum seekers in the UK and established communities.

Government and Policy

The publication of this Handbook is timely. There is growing concern about the perceived frailty of the social fabric of British society, about strained community relations and the need for what is broadly understood as 'cohesive communities'. The concept of 'community cohesion' emerged as a key policy concern following the 2001 disturbances in Burnley, Oldham and Bradford where there had been a clearly identified lack of interaction between individuals of different cultural, religious and racial backgrounds. Community cohesion was seen by the Government as crucial to promoting greater knowledge of, respect towards and contact between cultures, and to establishing a greater sense of citizenship.

The Home Office defines a cohesive community as one where:

- there is a common vision and a sense of belonging for all communities;
- the diversity of people's backgrounds and circumstances is appreciated and positively valued;
- those from different backgrounds have similar life opportunities; and
- strong and positive relationships are being developed between people from different backgrounds in the workplace, in schools and within neighbourhoods.

The former Home Secretary Charles Clark launched *Improving Opportunity, Strengthening Society: The Government's strategy to increase race equality and community cohesion* in January 2005. The strategy sets out how the Government will 'ensure that a person's ethnicity is not a barrier to their success' and 'foster the cohesion necessary to enable people from minority and majority communities to work together for social and economic progress'.

Much of the focus of UK Government policy has been on relations within and between established white and ethnic minority groups, and more recently the 'Muslim community' and newer groups, often referred to as the 'refugee and asylum seeker community'. This labelling of 'communities' is in itself problematic. Can groups of Zimbabweans, Somalis, and Colombians, comprising men and women, Muslims, Christians and different social classes all be seen as one community? Politicians, newsreaders and voluntary sector representatives use the term indiscriminately to cover a wide range of groups distinguished by nationality, class, gender, race, faith and ethnicity. If the notion of community is undefined then 'community cohesion' is equally open to interpretation. This is likely to raise problems for practitioners expected to achieve 'community cohesion' through their work.

Since 2000, the Government has settled newly arrived asylum seekers around the country under its 'dispersal' programme, designed to alleviate pressure on services in the south-east. Much of the accommodation for asylum seekers has been situated in inner-city neighbourhoods with existing economic and social problems, and among communities which often had little knowledge of their new neighbours or experience of dealing with newcomers. The dispersal programme has been criticised for failing adequately to take into account community-relations considerations when deciding on dispersal areas or in later plans to build accommodation centres for new arrivals in rural areas.

There have been reports of attacks against asylum seekers and protests by local residents about the proposed accommodation centres. Negative, mainly tabloid, media reporting on asylum, and the links some newspapers have made between immigration and the 'war on terror', have further heightened anxiety and raised the spectre that asylum seekers and other immigrants are adding to a generalised sense of insecurity. Initiatives from the recently created Home Office Community Cohesion Unit to generate a sense of national belonging among immigrants have included citizenship ceremonies and 'Britishness' tests for new Britons; Chancellor of the Exchequer Gordon Brown recently called for a 'Britain Day' to celebrate civic and national pride.

However, much of the emphasis on the settlement of asylum seekers and refugees has been directed towards how the migrant 'integrates' into the host community, mainly through accessing housing, health and employment, as opposed to how existing communities adjust to and accommodate migrants. The latest Government integration strategy, *Integration Matters*, offers little guidance on how to foster good relations, particularly from the point of view of supporting established local communities. Additionally, there is little evidence that relations between new and existing communities are integrated in mainstream social policy agendas, despite a wealth of recent policy initiatives to foster community well-being.

Finally, it is important to make a policy distinction between asylum seekers and refugees. Once a person is granted refugee status, a range of rights and support come into being, from permission to work to personal 'integration' support under the new Home Office Sunrise initiative.[1] For asylum seekers, who are prohibited from working whilst their cases are being considered, the focus is on temporary subsistence, not integration. Those who have remained in the country having failed in their application for refugee status, or have otherwise become destitute as a consequence of failing to apply in time, must also be living in established communities. If there is no expectation or incentive for people to contribute to their local community, it raises the question of how this affects community cohesion. More recently, the Government has removed 'indefinite' refugee status, making it subject to review, adding a new uncertainty for the integration of refugees.

Research and Thinking

Attitudes

If we assume that good relations between established communities and new migrants exist when people feel safe and secure, are included in and can contribute to community life, and interact positively and respectfully, then how is this to be achieved? What enables people to feel and act like this? What shapes public attitudes to others in society? And if people are negative towards the asylum system, asylum seekers and refugees, as evidence suggests, how can this be changed?

There is evidence to show that while established ethnic minority groups are viewed by the majority population as an accepted if not necessarily welcomed part of a multicultural society, hostility towards recently arrived immigrants has been growing.[2] Opinion polls over recent years suggest an overall negative view towards asylum seekers and refugees, and immigration more generally. Attitudes reflected in polls indicate that:

- people are very concerned that immigration is not under control;
- people question the genuineness of asylum seekers: asylum seekers are associated with illegality and deviance and are perceived to be economically motivated;
- the perceived numbers of asylum seekers entering the UK are seen to be a great problem;
- this, together with concern about the genuineness of asylum seekers, constitutes a threat to British society, including religion, values, ethnicity and health, and to the British economy, through criminality, increased competition and an economic burden;[3]
- people feel that asylum seekers are given preferential treatment and are better off than the average white Briton.[4]

A qualitative study, carried out by the Institute for Public Policy Research (IPPR), addressed similar issues. Research involving a number of interviews and focus groups in six UK locations suggested that hostility to asylum seekers has reached new levels. However, the research also highlighted public support for the principle of asylum.[5] Polls have shown that 78 per cent of people, and 89 per cent of ethnic minorities, think it is important to respect the rights of minorities[6] and 64 per cent of people think immigrants have benefited British society.[7]

Recent research on how public attitudes towards asylum seekers and refugees are influenced points to a number of interrelating factors. The current socio-political climate of uncertain national identity and national security is one, and while few studies have addressed the impact of the 'war on terror', IPPR has found negative attitudes towards asylum seekers, particularly Muslim asylum seekers who were often associated with terrorism.[8] Geographical variance indicates that attitudes are shaped by local experience of migration and of minority ethnic populations, including through dispersal, the existing sense of community, political traditions and economic history, and by local information networks including the local press.[9] For example, in a 2004 poll, a far smaller proportion of people in Scotland (57 per cent) compared to England and Wales (75 per cent) agreed with the statement 'Too many immigrants are coming to Britain.'[10]

Socio-economic status is another factor. Evidence suggests that the greater the inequalities in economic and social status, and the more intense the competition for resources, the more difficult it is for people to come together and bridge the gap that divides communities.[11]

Several recent studies have analysed media coverage, particularly press coverage, of asylum issues where asylum seekers have been perceived as problems or threats, with key themes being the reduction of migrant rights, the burden on the welfare state, and the dishonesty of migrants, although local press have tended to be more positive. In 2004 ICAR undertook a pilot study for the Greater London Authority (GLA) into the links between media coverage and community tensions. The study concluded that, in general, media images were found to be unbalanced and inaccurate and this was considered by community leaders and local residents to contribute towards community tension and the harassment of asylum seekers, although it was more likely to be influential where pre-existing attitudes were hostile.

The 'contact hypothesis' suggests that contact between members of different groups has the potential to break down fears and anxieties and may lead to greater understanding and tolerance. Research that has investigated relations between existing populations and newly arrived asylum seekers generally supports the notion that individual contact improves relations between people.[12] However, this depends on the type of contact, which can be negative as well as positive, and how 'meaningful' it is. Furthermore, a recent study of young people in the UK found that the attitudes of young people attending schools in multicultural areas revealed less not more tolerance than those living in less diverse areas.[13]

Other factors that affect public attitudes include demographics (age, sex, and race); psychological factors, such as personality type; political beliefs; and cultural factors, such as religion and ethnicity.[14]

What works?

The impact of negative attitudes is well documented. Asylum seekers and refugees fear harassment or attack while members of the host community fear harassment or crime from asylum seekers and refugees who, under some circumstances, may be perceived as threatening outsiders. Aside from a number of high-profile cases, such as the murder of a Kurdish asylum seeker on the Sighthill estate in Glasgow in 2001, research and monitoring suggests that the harassment of asylum seekers is a problem in some areas though it is unclear whether harassment is directed at asylum seekers as a category of people, or whether they experience generalised racial harassment.[15] The widely reported involvement of people with refugee status in terrorist activities in the UK, including the London bombings, has brought further challenges to those who seek to change perceptions and attitudes.

The creation of harmonious community relations is a considerable challenge and complex socio-economic problems remain. It would be unrealistic to expect the projects detailed in this Handbook to make significant inroads into such major structural problems. However, we might expect potentially successful projects to be aiming to meet some of the community cohesion objectives, such as encouraging relationships and building trust, by tackling identified problems, misinformation and lack of meaningful contact.

Current knowledge on this subject is limited and there is evidence that what knowledge is available has not been effectively disseminated to practitioners, who often ask for help with this aspect of their work. Contemporary studies that do exist on initiatives to build bridges between new and established communities share a number of findings. A finding of this Handbook is that while creating opportunities for contact between different groups is seen as important, it is the shared participation in tasks, rather than casual daily interactions, that is most likely to result in positive relations. An extensive study in the United States of America found that the one shared interest that persistently emerged as a rallying point for newcomers and established residents was characterised in the literature as initiatives aimed at 'controlling the character of community change'.[16] In these projects participants would mobilise around issues of security and quality of life, such as drugs, crime or the decline of public services. A situation that threatened everyone gave potential for people to meet, organise and work towards a common goal. Elsewhere it has been shown that doing 'community development' work across communities is effective only if the mixing of people is not treated as an end in itself but instead leads to a common goal that benefits all members of the community.[17] Paradoxically, however, it should be noted that the same socio-economic problems that bring people together also have the potential to divide them and scapegoat minorities. Hence the role of the community development worker is a critical one, in negotiating this contact and ensuring that the subject matter of the project is not in itself responsible for creating new tensions.

Building bridges is a two-way process and only works on the premise that both established residents and newcomers find ways of adjusting to and supporting one another. One-sided approaches, such as focusing on the assimilation of the migrant only, or not listening to concerns of receiving communities, are not seen to be conducive to good relations. Enabling both sides to change together without fear is more likely to foster healthy dynamics.[18] Though seemingly at odds with this, building the capacity of Refugee Community Organisations (RCOs), normally homogeneous associations based on nationality, faith or ethnicity, is increasingly seen as a prerequisite for bridging with the wider community. Although creating bonds within social groups has the potential to lead to self-segregation, as a means of fostering an initial sense of security from which links to other groups can then more confidently be made, this can provide an essential building block for good community relations.[19]

A recent study for the Commission for Racial Equality highlighted some of the key design aspects necessary for projects which aim to foster positive attitudes between established communities and asylum seekers and refugees. These included developing clear and realistic aims, basing approaches on recognised theories of attitude change, having sustained activities over a period of time, establishing good relations with the media and measuring impact.[20] Other work has pointed to the significance of core ingredients, such as key individuals, or 'brokers', who possess the personal attributes and commitment to build bridges between people, and of institutional support, such as the involvement of a local authority or a neighbourhood school.

While there is considerable interest in the impact of new migration, at least in the form of new research initiatives, there remains little in the way of policy or practical guidance. This may be in part because the development of 'good' community relations, and the influencing of opinion it entails, is a complex concept. Without clear direction about 'what works', projects have inevitably evolved in a piecemeal fashion, often responding to local circumstances. However, across the country people are working in different ways to build bridges between new and established groups. By showcasing recent local level initiatives, this Handbook is contributing to an emerging debate about the settlement of new migrants within Britain's established communities.

1. The Sunrise (Strategic Upgrade of National Refugee Integration Services) pilot projects provide new refugees with support from an allocated caseworker, who will 'help manage their transition from asylum seeker to refugee and help their early integration into life in the UK'. For more information refer to the Home Office website: http://www.ind.homeoffice.gov.uk
2. M. Lewis, *Asylum: Understanding public attitudes* (London, IPPR, 2005).
3. N. Finney, *Asylum Seeker Dispersal: Public attitudes and press portrayals around the UK* (University of Wales Swansea, PhD thesis, 2004).
4. G. Valentine and I. McDonald, *Understanding Prejudice: Attitudes towards minorities* (London, Stonewall, 2004) found that people believe asylum seekers, travellers and black people receive preferential treatment.
5. M. Lewis, *Asylum: Understanding public attitudes* (London, IPPR, 2005).
6. MORI/CRE, *The Voice of Britain: A research study conducted for the CRE by MORI* (London, MORI/CRE, 2002).
7. YouGov, *Immigration and Asylum survey* (prepared for *The Sun*, August 2003).
8. M. Lewis, *Asylum: Understanding public attitudes* (London, IPPR, 2005).
9. N. Finney, *Asylum Seeker Dispersal: Public attitudes and press portrayals around the UK* (University of Wales Swansea, PhD thesis, 2004).
10. YouGov/*The Economist*, *YouGov/Economist Survey Results* (December 2004)
11. A. Rudiger, 'Integration of New Migrants: Community relations' in S. Spencer, ed., *New Migrants and Refugees: Review of evidence on good practice* (Oxford, Oxford University Press, Forthcoming).
12. Greek Council for Refugees, *Good Practice Guide on the Integration of Refugees in the European Union: Community and culture* (Athens, European Council on Refugees and Exiles, 1999); M. Hollands, 'Upon Closer Acquaintance: The impact of direct contact with refugees on Dutch hosts', *Journal of Refugee Studies* 14(3), 2001, pp. 295–314; R.L. Hewitt, *Asylum Seeker Dispersal and Community Relations: An analysis of development strategies* (London, Goldsmith's College, University of London, 2002); H. Meert, K. Peleman and K. Stuyck, 'The Establishment of Asylum Centres: Creating a social basis for a dignified asylum policy', paper presented at the Annual Conference of the Royal Geographical Society (with The Institute of British Geographers), London, September 2003; N. Finney, *Asylum Seeker Dispersal: Public attitudes and press portrayals around the UK* (University of Wales Swansea, PhD thesis, 2004); L. D'Onofrio and K. Munk, *Understanding the Stranger: Final report* (London, ICAR, 2004).
13. G. Lemos, *The Search for Tolerance: Challenging and changing racist attitudes and behaviour among young people* (London, Joseph Rowntree Foundation, 2005).
14. For more on public attitude formation see: http://www.icar.org.uk
15. ICAR, *Media Image, Community Impact: Assessing the impact of media and political images of refugees and asylum seekers on community relations in London. Report of a pilot research study* (London, ICAR, 2004); A. Clark, *The Reporting and Recording of Racist Incidents Against Asylum Seekers in the North East of England* (Newcastle, University of Northumbria, 2004)
16. R. Bach, *et al.*, *Changing Relations: Newcomers and established residents in US communities* (New York, Ford Foundation, 1993).
17. A. Rudiger, 'Integration of New Migrants: Community relations' in S. Spencer, ed., *New Migrants and Refugees: Review of evidence on good practice* (Oxford, Oxford University Press, Forthcoming).
18. *Ibid*.
19. *Ibid*.
20. N. Finney and E. Peach, *Attitudes Towards Asylum Seekers, Refugees and Other Immigrants: A literature review for the Commission for Racial Equality* (London, CRE, 2004).

Methodology

In compiling this Handbook an extensive call for projects was sent out via a wide range of local, regional and national networks, through newsletters, websites and email groupings between April and October 2005. Interested individuals and groups were asked to send information about their work and to complete a case study profile form. The research team also searched relevant funder and organisational databases. In all, a database of 148 potential projects was compiled and direct contacts were made with as many of the projects as was practicable. Of those projects 48 were identified as potentially suitable and more detailed information was sought. From those projects, a structured sample of 21 was then selected for inclusion in the Handbook. The main criteria for selection were based on a need to present a range of projects from both the voluntary and statutory sectors. The projects were also geographically representative. And the projects explicitly stated as a central aim the improvement of relations between established communities and recently arrived asylum seekers and refugees where the community was identifiably divided.

The research team interviewed the project leaders, either by visiting the project location or by telephone, to gather information about the motivation for and evolution of the project, how it was undertaken, its outcomes and impact, and any lessons that were learned in the process. The interviews were transcribed and returned to the project staff to verify their accuracy and were subsequently analysed through a logical framework approach. The project-specific information was then edited according to a template from which the presentation of the projects in this Handbook has evolved. In this process, where necessary, additional information was sought from the interviewees.

Limitations and Exclusions

In order to present new ideas, projects were selected that have not been widely written about elsewhere.

While attempting to draw out key lessons to inform further thinking, case studies rely largely on self-reported data from one main source, which in most cases was the project leader, although occasionally it was possible to interview more than one person. Researchers did not interview beneficiaries of the initiatives and therefore the information presented does not reflect their assessment of quality or success. Wherever possible, project documentation was consulted, including any available evaluation reports, and incorporated into the study. The small-scale nature of many projects meant that they had not been formally evaluated. Arts-based projects have not been featured as these have recently been showcased in a Creative Exchange publication, *A Sense of Belonging*.

Categorisation

The case studies have been categorised under five headings. While some initiatives may cross over more than one subject area, they have been classified according to their main stated aims.

Community development
Focus is on the community as a whole and its capacity for self-determination

Developing responsive public services
Making public services more responsive to the impact of new immigration on existing communities

Increasing understanding
A direct approach to the issue of difference, normally involving a two-way exchange between established resident and newcomer

Local integration
Integrating newcomers, where the emphasis is on enabling asylum seekers and refugees through support, access and skills development

Personal development
Building the capacity of individuals in order that they can better understand, live and work with others

COMMUNITY DEVELOPMENT

1 Leicester North West Community Forum

The Project
Leicester North West Community Forum is a resident-run, not-for-profit, regeneration initiative that recruits and trains local residents to take active roles in improving the local community and provides a platform for residents to influence local government and business leaders. It has a specialist staff member whose role it is to involve refugees and asylum seekers in the work of the Forum.

It has been designated a 'Guide Neighbourhood' by the Home Office Civil Renewal Unit. Guide Neighbourhoods are successful community organisations which have tackled issues such as crime, poor housing and unemployment in their community and which look to the residents themselves to take the initiative and bring about the changes needed.

Background
Leicester has the largest number of people of Indian origin in any local authority area in England and Wales. Government statistics in 2005 documented approximately 950 asylum seekers in Leicester but there is no data on the number of refugees. The north-west of the city includes two wards where the population is amongst the 10 per cent most deprived in the UK. Over 20 per cent of this population are from ethnic minorities.

Why do it?
Community leaders reported a growing and negative concern about the number of asylum seekers being dispersed to the neighbourhood. Negative coverage in the local press was not helping the situation. It was felt that two immediate issues existed: dealing with the needs of the new arrivals and circulating accurate information among the host community.

Key Concerns

Locals
That newcomers were 'taking our jobs', getting free benefits as well as furnished houses.

Newcomers
Were worried about their future, their safety and racism.

Approach and Activities

- 'Listening times': street-level discussions where established and new residents are invited to listen to information from the Forum's refugee worker about asylum seekers and refugees
- Drop-in sessions where newcomers can come for advice and information
- 'Patch walks' where Forum members, local business leaders, local councillors and the police walk around the neighbourhood each month and meet groups of residents at prearranged points to hear concerns
- A welcome pack for new arrivals to the area
- 'Integration workshops' to give newcomers information about services, laws and entitlements
- Leadership training for identified 'good neighbours' or those who wish to become active volunteer community workers
- 'Awareness-raising' sessions at schools, churches and tenants association meetings
- Organised trips to activity centres for mixed groups of locals and newcomers

The overall approach is to involve the whole community in improving the neighbourhood through shared participation in community events and leadership training. There is also an element of awareness raising through information on the real-life situation of refugees and asylum seekers.

The project bases its work on a six-phase approach, which, using a combination of the activities listed above, includes initial contact and engagement with newly arrived asylum seekers and refugees, personal capacity building, awareness raising of established residents, integrated community events, community capacity building and finally 'civil renewal'.

Aims

- Integration
- Building trust
- Getting refugees and asylum seekers involved in community decision-making

Achievements

- Refugees and asylum seekers feel more confident and welcome
- The Forum has trained 60 volunteers to be 'good neighbours' of which 25 are refugees and asylum seekers
- Good relations have been created between new and established residents
- A mixed refugee and locals women's group has been created
- The whole community has become more involved in neighbourhood issues

How do we know?
- Statistical data on the numbers of people trained, seeking advice and attending events
- The observations of the Forum staff

What Made a Difference?

Internal factors

The Forum is led by a committee of 12 elected volunteers from the neighbourhood, of which three are from refugee backgrounds.

External factors

The local media was negative at first but is reporting more positively since the Forum's work with refugees and asylum seekers began.

Key Messages

- The community will do things for itself if you let it
- Work from the bottom up
- Partnership is very important – 'we couldn't have done the work alone'

Facts and Figures

- The Home Office Civil Renewal Unit as part of the Together We Can action plan is funding Guide Neighbourhoods to pass on the lessons they have learnt to other community groups who want to tackle similar issues
- At the present time the Home Office is funding 10 Guide Neighbourhoods nationally
- The Forum is funded by the Home Office Civil Renewal Unit, the Single Regeneration Budget, the European Community Fund, Metropolitan Housing Trust and the Neighbourhood Renewal Fund
- The Forum started in 2000; the refugee work started in 2004
- Up to 40 refugees and asylum seekers access the Forum offices every week
- 60 established residents and new refugee and asylum seekers have been trained as 'good neighbours'
- Collaborating organisations include: the Refugee Housing Association, Sure Start, the police, the NHS, local churches, schools, tenants associations, local businesses and Leicester City Council
- The Forum has five paid staff led by a residents' committee of both established residents and people from refugee backgrounds

Contact

Jean-Didier Mualaba
Refugee Community Development Worker
Leicester North West Community Forum
Alchemy House, 90–2 Bishopdale Road
Beaumont Leys
Leicester LE4 0SR
Tel: 0116 229 3206
E-mail: jean.didier@alchemyhouse.co.uk

COMMUNITY DEVELOPMENT

2 Refugee Accommodate Project, Canopy Housing

The Project
Run by Canopy Housing, the Refugee Accommodate Project brings volunteers from local host and asylum-seeking and refugee communities together to refurbish derelict and disused houses to provide housing for refugees and homeless locals. Inspired by its sister project, a general needs initiative in Hyde Park, Leeds, it has been working with refugees since April 2005.

Background
The project is situated in the Beeston Hill area of Leeds, an urban renewal area commonly associated with racial tension, a degree of community isolation, and urban decline. Though lacking in investment, Beeston Hill is regarded as a vibrant part of the city. There is a lot of street life, people know and talk to one other. There are high levels of long-term unemployment and the poor condition of housing and low levels of personal aspiration are identified as major problems. Refugees and asylum seekers are new to the area but are becoming a significant element in the community. There is a white working class community and a large established Asian population.

Why do it?
Canopy's first project in Hyde Park was set up in response to the large numbers of boarded-up properties in the area, local young people's exclusion from school, and homelessness. The project proposed bringing these factors together in schemes to renovate housing. The project team noticed that some of those volunteering were refugees and were keen to meet their specific needs in recognition of the importance to them of 'home'. Canopy had also been referred homeless refugees from hostels. Funding was sought to replicate the Hyde Park project in Beeston Hill.

Approach and Activities
Canopy is run as a volunteer programme that involves 60–70 people a year in the refurbishment of derelict properties. Most volunteers are from disadvantaged groups such as the unemployed, people excluded from schools and referrals from hostels. Each house refurbishment is carried out by a team, but the person who will occupy the property has control over how it is decorated. The potential tenant receives a support package during the 10–12 week volunteering phase when help is given with integration into the local area, with welfare advice and access to formal training opportunities. The project office acts as an open resource for tenants and volunteers to access help and support, facilities and social opportunities.

The overall approach is one of shared engagement in local regeneration, where the main aim is to renew local resources for the benefit of both newcomers and established residents and where the building of relationships is an important part of the process.

The Beeston project provides opportunities for homeless people as well as refugees to create their own home, and in this way ensures that the beneficiaries of the project remain a mixed group and the refugees are not isolated or seen as 'special cases'. The idea is to engage excluded groups in a practical task of mutual benefit. Canopy hopes that through working together, stereotypes might be broken down, but this is not a primary aim of the project. Almost all discussion of refugee issues in general or of people's specific circumstances occurs on a one-to-one basis as people get to know each other and become friends.

The project emphasises practicality, informality, building a sense of belonging and having fun. Where attitude-related issues came up they were addressed through open-house discussions.

Aims

- To engage disadvantaged and marginalised people in the improvement of the inner-city built environment, thereby helping the individual to realise both his/her own and the area's potential
- To work with homeless people – including refugees – in the renovation of disused properties to create homes that are secure, affordable and decent
- To bring together newly arrived refugees and the local community to contribute towards the regeneration of the Beeston Hill area of Leeds and foster a sense of community cohesion

Achievements

- Seven refugees have completed their homes since the project started in April 2005
- The project has helped to create a sense of community
- It has helped provide a route back into work-based activity and engaged previously isolated people
- Asylum seekers and refugees have made friends within the volunteer group, improving their English and knowledge of the area and creating their own home

How do we know?
From appraisals and reviews with volunteers and tenants.

What Made a Difference?

Internal factors
- It is an informal, participatory and practical approach that is supportive and inclusive
- Everyone is encouraged to take a role
- There are effective partnerships with local schools, refugee agencies, housing associations and the local authority
- There is a cautious approach to the press: Canopy is as wary about the press wanting to write a positive story of 'refugee integration' as it is about negative coverage. The project wants a track record on regenerating houses and local approval before it thinks about media coverage

External factors
- It operates in a regeneration area
- There is support from the local authority and larger social housing providers in helping to obtain disused properties

Key Messages

- It is promoted as a local regeneration project that provides an opportunity to learn practitioner skills, rather than as a 'community cohesion' project
- Relationships are allowed to develop in a natural way whilst working together on joint projects

Facts and Figures

- Canopy works with 60–70 volunteers a year
- About 20–30 per cent of the volunteers involved in the Beeston project are refugees or asylum seekers
- The Beeston Hill project was developed with the help of a grant from the Housing and Charitable Trust's national Accommodate programme, which provided funding to employ a worker for six months to help develop the idea. This worker was herself a refugee who had been able to access housing through the Hyde Park project. Further funding was received from the Camelot Foundation, Leeds City Council and Leeds South Homes
- The project is ongoing and aims to renovate between six and eight houses per year
- An external evaluation by Birmingham University is underway
- The Empty Homes Agency gave Canopy its national award for Community Action on Empty Properties
- In total, Canopy has brought back into use 30 disused and derelict properties

Contact

Mark Stevens
Project Co-ordinator
Refugee Accommodate Project
Canopy Housing
66 Burley Lodge Rd
Leeds LS6 1QF
Tel: 0113 274 8318
E-mail: canopy.housing@ntworld.com

Quotes

'It's not a social experiment. The approach is much more informal and Canopy is wary of creating an 'us' and 'them' scenario and of labelling or lecturing either group. Equal opportunities and cultural awareness training for all volunteers is being considered but Canopy is not keen to make this too formal.'

'The usual myths inevitably surface from time to time but disappear again as people mix and work together.'
Mark Stevens, Project Co-ordinator

Refugee Accomodate Project, Canopy Housing

DEVELOPING RESPONSIVE PUBLIC SERVICES

3 Camden Scrutiny Panel, Camden Council

The Project
In 2002, Camden councillors formed a Scrutiny Panel to assess the situation facing refugees and asylum seekers in the borough, particularly with regard to employment. Made up of councillors from all three main political parties, it collected and reviewed evidence from a variety of local sources. This led to the development of a number of successful work strands to benefit both local refugee and asylum-seeking and host communities.

Background
The London Borough of Camden has a diverse population of 217,000 which has grown by 8 per cent in five years. Around 27 per cent are from ethnic minorities, with Bangladeshis making up the largest group. Of the estimated 25,000 refugees in the borough, there are significant numbers of Somalis, Congolese and Kosovans. There have been a number of 'community cohesion' initiatives over the years.

Why do it?
The growth of new communities from refugee and asylum-seeking backgrounds, and an awareness of the negative employment experiences of these groups in Camden, led to the Council's equalities unit proposing the work as part of its commitments under its social inclusion and race equality strategy. The cross-party Overview and Scrutiny Panel took on this responsibility and chose employment as the focus for the panel in response to arguments that refugees were 'undeserving'. The aim was to publicise evidence relating to the extent of skills among refugees, their levels of underemployment and the potential contributions they could make to society.

Key Concerns
Locals
Firstly, the perception that asylum seekers and refugees are getting preferential access to affordable housing, and secondly that they are putting pressure on health services. A further concern is that the notion of 'Britishness' as an identity is being challenged by new immigration.

Newcomers
The Scrutiny Panel worked on the assumption that the main needs for refugees and asylum seekers are housing and subsistence followed by education and employment.

Approach and Activities
- The collection of evidence from council officers and relevant agencies such as the Refugee Council, World University Service, Refugee Community Organisations (RCOs) and the Medical Foundation
- The Scrutiny Panel met once a month between October 2002 and June 2003 to review evidence gathered
- Individual meetings with refugees and asylum seekers: they were invited through public notices and letters in community languages to speak at panel meetings or more informal sessions
- Dissemination of a final report and recommendations
- Local media coverage of the findings

The overall approach was to use information about the real-life situation of refugees and asylum seekers to break down misconceptions and raise awareness amongst councillors, council staff and the local public and through this influence local policy. The panel found there was little hard evidence about the conditions in which refugees and asylum seekers lived. By 'making the case', the work of the panel helped break down public misconceptions and gave a business argument for greater attention to relevant issues in the borough. Having a specific and positive focus (employment and the labour market), from which concrete proposals could be made, avoided moving into wider and potentially negative discussions, including the economic 'cost' of new immigration. Importantly, cross-party political support ensured there was the political will to instigate change. The work of the Scrutiny Panel acted as a catalyst and stimulated activities that otherwise may not have happened. The engagement of refugees in the process, the first time this had been done by the Council, ensured real-life experiences were heard.

Aims
To alleviate the problems of unemployment and underemployment amongst refugee and asylum-seeking communities within a broader strategy of social inclusion.

Achievements
- The work of the panel provided an evidence base which the Council used to attract further funding for refugee and asylum-seeker work. This included a work placement scheme in public libraries and a job brokerage and training project
- By bringing together councillors from the three main parties, the panel achieved local political commitment to promote positive messages about refugees and asylum seekers
- Positive images about the contribution of refugees and asylum seekers appeared in the local press
- The work has increased understanding about the local refugee and asylum-seeker population amongst council staff
- Camden Council has been promoted in a number of national conferences and reports as a model borough because of this work, raising the profile of local authorities and their potential for innovative work with new communities

How do we know?
The final recommendations and subsequent progress are reviewed each year by the Overview and Scrutiny Commission and the Camden Refugee Forum, a local multi-agency network.

What Made a Difference?
Internal factors
- Getting councillors together from different ends of the political spectrum, though challenging, also gave the panel strength
- The time and commitment of the panel members, including the chair, a Conservative councillor, who worked hard to see the process through and was passionate in putting recommendations to the council
- Engaging refugees and RCOs was difficult as most had little experience of dealing with local authorities

External factors
Generally the local media was quite positive. There are frequent 'human interest' stories about particular individuals or households.

Key Messages
- Commitment from all members ensured success
- Promoting the economic contribution of refugees and asylum seekers made the work politically marketable

Facts and Figures
- Overview and Scrutiny Commissions are cross-party bodies of councillors whose functions are, amongst others, to hold the executive to account, review and develop policy, review best value, engage partner organisations, the public and the press
- The panel was set up in August 2002 and published its final report in July 2003
- Funding came from the Council's internal resources
- Camden is referred to as a model of good practice in the IPPR report, *Asylum: Understanding public attitudes* (2005)
- Recommendations from the panel led to the Council securing £1.5 million from the European Social Fund to run the RAISE project (Refugees Access into Sustainable Employment), which provides ESOL, training, job brokerage, and RCO capacity building

Contact
George Binette
Equalities Officer
Camden Town Hall
Judd Street
London WC1H 9JE
Tel 020 7278 4444
E-mail: george.binette@camden.gov.uk
Website: www.camden.gov.uk

Information also provided by: Vickie Skade, Policy Officer

Quotes
'It's an ongoing process, not a finished piece of work.'
George Binette, Camden Equalities Officer and adviser to the panel

DEVELOPING RESPONSIVE PUBLIC SERVICES

4 Community Outreach Team and the New Communities Team, Southampton City Council

The Project
The Community Outreach Team (COT) is concerned primarily with reacting to and attempting to decrease the likelihood of community tension between different ethnic and/or religious groups in the city and the New Communities Team (NCT) focuses on developing a proactive long-term city-wide integration strategy for new communities, including European Union (EU) accession state migrant communities. The approach is about enabling community involvement and developing appropriate mainstream services.

Background
Southampton has a history of immigration, yet the number of newcomers into the area has increased dramatically in recent years as a result of asylum dispersal policy and EU accession. There has also been proactive international recruitment in the area to fill local vacancies. Increasingly, families with refugee status have chosen to stay in the city. There is, therefore, a wide range of communities in the area. The main inter-community conflict has been between new migrant communities and established black and minority ethnic (BME) residents.

Why do it?
The COT was formed in response to a civil disturbance in March 2002 between established BME residents and asylum-seeking populations. The NCT evolved out of the work of the COT in order to look more strategically at new communities' integration needs. The evidence for this came from a COT conference for new refugee communities in October 2003. This brought together key agencies and new communities to enable better understanding of each others' cultures, ways of working, needs and services.

Key Concerns
Locals
Local BME communities in particular were concerned about long-term social problems such as unemployment and substance abuse. Asylum issues had become a channel through which to air these frustrations.

Newcomers
The main concerns were unemployment, housing and education, English proficiency and feeling excluded from the community.

Approach and Activities
- Inter-communal dialogue in the form of community mediation
- Building capacity amongst new communities by supporting organisations, groups and networks
- Information gathering to identify the needs of new communities
- Networking and information sharing between statutory and voluntary sector organisations about how to meet the needs of new communities

Building the capacity of individuals and groups to enable new communities to lead their own networks and organisations is central to both projects. This encourages community involvement, though it does not necessarily mean creating more organisations. Both projects, however, are based on the belief that integrating newcomers more effectively reduces potential for community conflict.

Both projects developed a team of workers with knowledge and experience of the communities targeted by the project. This team then forged links with these communities to establish a dialogue and enable participation.

Aims

- COT – To work very closely with new and established communities throughout the city to improve cross-cultural understanding, alert agencies to the possibility of serious tensions and potential conflict and to facilitate improved community cohesion
- NCT – To develop and implement a mainstream, inter-agency, city-wide integration strategy for new communities

Achievements

- A coherent strategy driving integration in the area
- Attendance at meetings and contributions from new communities on the strategy
- Improved information networks between new communities and mainstream agencies

How do we know?

From outreach workers' contact with communities and information exchange with partner agencies.

What Made a Difference?

Internal factors

- A strategy that focused on forging good links with host communities to keep them informed
- Enabling capacity to emerge organically from within a community
- Having a team of outreach workers added value and credibility to the wider strategy of the two projects

External factors

- The length of time a community had been established – for example for the recently arrived Kurdish community, building community groups takes time, money and effort
- Intra- and inter-community dynamics

Key Messages
- Community capacity building takes time and expectations are often raised beyond what it is realistic to achieve
- Host communities need to be prepared for and informed about new communities before they arrive
- Housing policy is central to ensuring good community relations

Facts and Figures
- COT and NCT are funded by the local authority
- COT is line managed by the Social Cohesion Team and is governed by a community steering group. NCT is situated in the City Council Asylum Team
- COT was established in November 2002
- COT comprises a full-time manager and a number of part-time outreach workers
- NCT evolved out of the COT in late 2003
- NCT has two full-time and two part-time staff

Contact
Gavin Barker
Community Outreach Team
Southampton City Council
Gateway House
39–45 Bernard Street
Southampton SO14 3NL
Tel: 023 8091 5477
E-mail: gavin.barker@southampton.gov.uk

Information also provided by: Tony Pascoe, NCT Manager and Abdul Mohammed, outreach worker.

Quotes
'There needs to be a strategy and good links with the host community to ensure they are prepared for and informed about the arrival of new communities.'
COT and NCT staff

DEVELOPING RESPONSIVE PUBLIC SERVICES

5 Regional Community Cohesion Project, North West Asylum Seekers Consortium

The Project
Based at the North West (East) Asylum Seekers Consortium (NWASC), the Community Cohesion Project supports and carries out the work of the Community Cohesion Strategic Forum, initially a joint initiative between the NWASC, Refugee Action and Greater Manchester Police. This is a strategic body bringing together key stakeholders to discuss community cohesion issues, give and share information and share practice and ideas.

Background
The Community Cohesion Project covers ten Greater Manchester local authorities, including Blackburn with Darwen in Lancashire. The area has changed significantly since the arrival of large numbers of asylum seekers under the Government's dispersal programme. However, this has been seen as marked by a lack of strategic planning, insensitive to local needs and services and more contingent on accommodation procurement, leading to pressure on local schools and other essential services.

Why do it?
A number of related factors gave rise to the need for a regional strategic intervention:

- various reports from 2001 onwards highlighted tensions in regional dispersal areas between new and established communities; there were further studies on community tensions in Oldham, Burnley and Bradford;
- the rise of far-right activities in the region since 2000;
- feedback from Consortium members about growing tension between locals and incoming asylum seekers and refugees.

Key Concerns

Locals
- Community stability and tensions
- Pressure on local services
- The policy of dispersal

Newcomers
- Lack of understanding of the local culture and customs
- Racism
- Crime

Approach and Activities
- Forum meetings with invited speakers
- Compilation and distribution of statistical information on racist incidents and hate crime, as reported by local authorities and accommodation providers for the National Asylum Support Service (NASS)

- Dissemination of research, reports and good practice examples relating to racism, hate crime and community cohesion
- Training local authority support workers on issues regarding racism, hate crime and reporting
- Establishment of a new regional database to help monitor racist incidents

The main approach is the use of information to make services more knowledgeable about asylum issues and better equipped to deal with community tensions, thereby reducing them.

The sharing and monitoring of information, ideas and good practice improve the approach of voluntary and statutory sector partners. Local authorities are encouraged to put out myth-busting information to the local community, organise days out for mixed groups of locals and newcomers and join the Greater Manchester Media Group to encourage positive asylum reporting. Better monitoring and reporting of hate crime gives the police and other agencies the information needed to tackle community tensions and be aware of race-crime hot spots.

Aims
- To reduce hostility towards refugees and asylum seekers by encouraging the reporting of racist incidents and hate crime involving asylum seekers and refugees across the region
- To increase awareness and knowledge about refugees and asylum seekers amongst statutory and voluntary agencies who were not fully prepared for dispersal
- To promote asylum-seeker and refugee issues positively, through local communities and the co-ordination of media strategies

Achievements
- New racist incident reporting methods and the mapping of local race-crime hot spots
- Increased reporting of race-hate crime amongst refugees and asylum seekers
- Increased awareness of the importance of reporting hate crime
- The development of a network of agencies
- Greater co-ordination between key statutory and voluntary organisations

How do we know?
From feedback from Forum members.

What Made a Difference?

Internal factors
- The Forum fitted into the structure of the existing NWASC
- Links already existed with key stakeholders through NWASC and it was therefore best placed to deliver the Forum and project
- Good attendance and commitment by members, especially the police, was essential

External factors
- It was felt that mixed Government messages produce a lack of clarity for the public. Current immigration policy goes against a welcoming culture

- Lack of understanding amongst the general public of the difference between asylum seekers, refugees, immigrant or migrant workers
- Dispersal has been viewed as badly planned and managed

Key Messages
- Local managers, such as local authority asylum managers, are best placed and informed to deliver this kind of work
- Many local authorities already have a community cohesion remit. It is better to make use of existing structures than reinvent or duplicate new ones
- More guidance needs to be given to projects that have a strategic rather than a frontline focus on how to monitor and evaluate their work

Facts and Figures
- The NWASC (East) and (West) are multi-agency bodies which have responsibility for co-ordinating the arrival and integration of asylum seekers and refugees in the North West of England
- The Consortium's Community Cohesion Strategic Forum was originally set up in October 2003
- The Community Cohesion Project started in December 2004. It ceases as a stand-alone project in 2006 but its activities will be carried forward by the NWASC, the police and Greater Manchester Against Crime
- The project is run by two paid staff, a Community Cohesion Officer and an administrator
- The main project partners are: ten Greater Manchester Local Authority Asylum Support Teams plus Blackburn with Darwen, Manchester Housing, Government Office for the North West, the Immigration Service, the National Asylum Support Service, Northwest Regional Development Agency, Clearsprings, Greater Manchester Police, Bedspace, Lancashire Police, Refugee Action, and Oldham Community Empowerment Team
- It is funded by the Home Office Challenge Fund

Contact
Emma Read
Community Cohesion Officer
NWASC
Northwest Consortium
9–11 Copthorne Crescent
Longsight
Manchester M13 0RA
Tel: 0161 248 0408
E-mail: emma.read@manchester.gov.uk

DEVELOPING RESPONSIVE PUBLIC SERVICES

6 Walsall Wardens Scheme

The Project
The Walsall Wardens Scheme is hosted by a partnership body: Walsall Housing Regeneration Agency (WHRA). The scheme employs wardens who act as community 'linkers', by promoting community safety and development. The scheme began working with refugees and asylum seekers in 2003 by developing a series of mini projects.

Background
This scheme is situated in Walsall, which has a population of 268,000. Thirteen per cent of this population is black and minority ethnic (BME). There are approximately 350 asylum seekers or refugees in Walsall, most of whom live in the Pleck neighbourhood.

Why do it?
Asylum seekers began arriving in Walsall in 2000 as a result of the Government's dispersal programme. The Walsall Wardens Scheme sought to work with existing partners to help to address the difficulties faced by asylum seekers and refugees living in the Walsall area. More broadly, it was recognised that there was a need to reduce the fear of crime, improve the quality of life for residents and increase community cohesion in the area.

Key Concerns
Locals
That refugee and asylum seekers are jumping the housing queue and getting luxuries.

Newcomers
- Language barriers
- Acceptance and orientation
- Poor accommodation
- The threat of homelessness after receiving refugee status

Approach and Activities
The specialised work carried out by wardens to help asylum seekers and refugees includes:

- relationship building – being a 'friendly face' on the street;
- meeting new families and linking them to services e.g. accessing GPs, training, English language training;
- introducing refugees and asylum seekers to community groups and local families;
- signposting young refugees and asylum seekers to local youth clubs.

In addition, five mini projects were established to meet the needs of refugees and asylum seekers in the area:

- a refugee information leaflet, with listings of services for housing, health education and training;
- Welcome Packs – these were translated into the five most commonly used languages and included an orientation booklet entitled *Living in Britain*;

- English language training for asylum seekers and refugees;
- a networking event for asylum seekers and refugees;
- access to recreational activities via sports projects – football coaching courses for both the host community and refugees and asylum seekers.

Aims
- To reduce the fear of crime and improve the quality of life for local communities
- To help breakdown the barriers faced by asylum seekers and refugees living in Walsall

Achievements
- A networking event attended by 200 people
- Getting stakeholders, such as local mosques, involved

How do we know?
- The scheme has been evaluated and the project has received letters of support
- Regionally and nationally the project has been heralded as an example of good practice
- Examples of how asylum seekers and refugees have been helped by the wardens have been recorded as case studies

What Made a Difference?

Internal factors

- Trying to identify and engage with those most isolated in the community was challenging
- The scheme received additional funding to employ a warden responsible for liaising with ethnic minority groups and this helped to further the work with refugees and asylum seekers

Key Messages

Regular communication and feedback from residents is important.

Facts and Figures

- The neighbourhood warden scheme began in 1999. There are now 500 schemes nationwide, with 41 in the West Midlands
- The Walsall scheme was established in 2001 and now employs more than 40 staff
- The project is jointly funded by the Office of the Deputy Prime Minister Grant Programme and the Neighbourhood Renewal Fund
- The networking event in March 2004 was attended by 40 asylum seekers and 20 local organisations

Contact

Natalie Jones
Co-ordinator
West Midlands Wardens and Neighbourhood Resource Centre
35 King Street
Darlaston
West Midlands WS10 8DD
Tel: 0121 526 6176
E-mail: natalie@whra.walsall.org.uk

Information also provided by: Bashir Ahmed, Head of Walsall Wardens, Yasmeen Nawaz, BME Worker and Abdul Kalam, Operations Manager.

Quotes

'Use wardens if they are in your area, they are a great source of intelligence and act as community linkers, contributing to the 'respect' agenda and community cohesion at a grass roots level.'
Staff member

7 Welcome to Your Library, London Libraries Development Agency

The Project
This project has a pilot and a national phase. The pilot aimed to identify and then devise strategies for tackling barriers restricting the access of refugees and asylum seekers to public libraries. The project also looked at how public libraries could develop their services to be more appropriate for refugees and asylum seekers. More broadly, the project addressed how libraries could contribute to an improved cultural understanding between different communities.

Background
The pilot project took place in five London boroughs: Brent, Camden, Enfield, Merton and Newham, with the national project currently in the process of being developed. Each borough is ethnically diverse by national standards. Newham is the most diverse with a black and minority ethnic (BME) population of around 60 per cent. The five boroughs are responsible for around 17 per cent of all asylum seekers supported by local authorities in Greater London.

Why do it?
The project was designed to encourage and enable public libraries to understand and act on their potential to play a key role in the community. The project drew on pioneering work with refugees and asylum seekers by the London Borough of Merton's Library and Heritage Service. The project responded to Government policy priorities for the integration of refugees, but also for the role of public libraries, and fitted with the London Libraries Development Agency's wider social inclusion agenda.

Approach and Activities
- Providing opportunities, such as storytelling, to bring different groups together
- Sessions to explain what the library can offer to refugees and asylum seekers and how its services can be accessed
- Simplifying joining procedures to enable more refugees and asylum seekers to become registered users
- Work placement schemes for refugees and asylum seekers in public libraries

At a strategic, national level the project was about understanding the role of the library in the community and its position in society as a space for community interaction. Initially the projects collected local community profile data to assess the size, location and make-up of refugee and asylum seeker communities in the area and to develop a realistic expectation of the effect this project could feasibly have. Library staff were also given training in refugee and asylum seeker issues. New collections and resources were made available in the libraries so that their stock was more relevant and appropriate for refugees and asylum seekers. The project was also monitored and evaluated.

Aims

Develop activities and approaches to improve access and information services for refugees and asylum seekers by:

- achieving sustainability;
- piloting at least one new initiative per borough;
- developing internal and external partnerships to support library work with refugees and asylum seekers;
- making recommendations for future projects;
- increasing awareness of and participation in library services among refugees and communities.

Achievements

- For refugees and asylum seekers: simplified procedures, linking of other facilities, increased familiarity with the library, engagement in integration activities and increased library membership
- For Refugee Community Organisations (RCOs): more engagement in planning services and opportunities to train library staff
- For library services: detailed data about refugee and asylum-seeker communities and their needs, new networks and improved staff skills
- For Local Authorities: access to detailed data, opportunities for complimentary service delivery
- For library policy bodies: the project provided an example of good practice and an enhanced profile for libraries within the community

How do we know?
- Monitoring through project diaries
- Project officer and co-ordinators wrote self-evaluation reports
- An Advice Development Project was commissioned to undertake an independent evaluation

What Made a Difference?

Internal factors
- The effectiveness of evidence gathering to strengthen the project's case, particularly at a policy level
- The involvement of refugee and other community and voluntary sector organisations in advising on service development
- The cumulative effect of working with several local authorities simultaneously, which meant that more learning and more momentum were generated

External factors
The project accorded with and was supported by Government policy. The Department for Culture Media and Sport's *Framework for the Future: Libraries Learning and Information for the Next Decade* (February 2003) sets out three priorities for public libraries including: 'measures to tackle social exclusion, build community identity and develop citizenship'. This was the backdrop for the project and made sure it was not acting in isolation.

Key Messages
- Public library staff need support to carry out these types of activity
- Trust needs to be developed with refugee and asylum-seeking communities to encourage participation
- Longer, more strategic projects are necessary to drive home the 'social argument' for mainstreaming the approach and work of the project – this requires funding

Facts and Figures
- The pilot project was devised by the London Development Agency (LDA) which is now managing the development of the national project
- Both stages of the project have been funded by the Paul Hamlyn Foundation
- The national project employs a full-time project co-ordinator, a position funded until November 2007
- The pilot project involved five London boroughs and the national project involves five public library services, two further London boroughs and three partners outside London

Contact
Helen Carpenter
Project Co-ordinator
London Libraries Development Agency
35 St Martin's Street
London WC2H 7HP
Tel: 020 7641 5266
E-mail: welcome@llda.org.uk
Website: www.llda.org.uk

Quotes
'Participation in the Welcome to Your Library project may be an expression of good will and good intentions on the part of a library service, but it also needs to be accompanied by an awareness of the barriers that some groups face in accessing a service like the public library.'

'Public library staff need to understand the importance of not making the registration procedure too official, but at the same time not giving the impression to other public library staff or users that refugees/asylum seekers are getting special treatment.'
Helen Carpenter, Project Co-ordinator

INCREASING UNDERSTANDING

8 Cooking Project, Centrepoint

The Project
Centrepoint runs foyers and services for young people aged 16–24 in London. The cooking project was part of an attempt to increase the participation of resident young people in tenants' meetings and other activities. A one-off initiative in 2004, it comprised a series of themed tenants' meetings which focused on residents' countries of origin. Young people were encouraged to cook food from their region and initiate a discussion about their country, culture and customs.

Background
Centrepoint's Bruce House is a hostel for homeless young people in the heart of Central London. At the time of the project more than 70 per cent of the 49 tenants were from asylum-seeking, refugee or immigrant backgrounds, the remainder being from white and ethnic minority British backgrounds. The surrounding area is mainly non-residential.

Why do it?
The 'usual suspects' were coming to tenants meetings and engaging with staff and activities while others, and in particular refugees and asylum seekers, were staying in their rooms, not participating. There was a concern that these young people were feeling isolated. As Bruce House is located in an area where there is only a weak sense of 'local community', it was important to build one up within the hostel.

Key Concerns

Non-refugee residents
Concerns are for their own needs. Little begrudging of refugees' and asylum seekers' presence.

Newcomers
The struggle to maintain practices and beliefs.

Approach and Activities
A series of themed events/meetings lasting two to three hours were held over six months, accompanied by food, music and a discussion on custom, religion and culture from a particular region of the world. Staff approached young people in the hostel and invited them to make a presentation about their region. They were given money to buy the necessary ingredients. This often involved the residents travelling to different areas of the city where they could find people and shops from their own community. The meetings were facilitated by the service manager but participants took over the discussion. Meeting themes were promoted through posters designed by the young people and put up around the hostel. Staff participated also by helping with the cooking and organising. Food was considered to be the main draw as this is the one thing that is guaranteed to bring the residents out of their rooms.

The approach was to celebrate and learn about difference through the sharing of food. This was achieved by validating each young person's experience, giving them an opportunity to show off their own country, its food, music, culture and history. In some senses, a level playing field was created as everyone's background and experience, including that of the British-born residents, was equally important.

Aims
- To increase participation in tenants' meetings
- To target and interest marginalised young people who were not engaging in the service, especially refugees and asylum seekers
- To build a sense of community in the service and encourage the forming of social networks

Achievements
- The project bonded the community and improved the atmosphere in Bruce House compared to other houses
- Staff started thinking about how diverse the residents were and this led to a cultural needs assessment of all residents
- It significantly improved communication, trust and therefore relations between staff and young people
- Young people felt really proud to share their culture and everyone became more educated about other cultures and countries
- There was increased engagement of refugees and asylum seekers; they made their voices heard
- It created new friendships

How do we know?
Mostly from staff observation of changed behaviour.

What Made a Difference?
- From the outset, direct cajoling of young people: phoning from room to room and encouraging participation
- The participation of staff gave a positive message to the young people. One Nigerian staff member helped with the cooking of Nigerian food. Young people saw their support workers in a new light because they joined in, so winning their trust

Key Messages
- Community building occurs when there are joint activities
- People enjoy talking about where they come from
- Educating each other about culture and background needs to be part of the agenda

Facts and Figures
- Bruce House has 49 young people aged 16–24
- Meetings comprised between 10 and 12 young people and showcased food and culture from East Africa, West Africa, the Caribbean, India, Turkey and the UK
- The project took place over a six-month period in 2004
- It led to the first 'community profile' being undertaken at Centrepoint, which assessed the diverse cultural backgrounds and needs of all Bruce House residents

- Discussion of the project for this Handbook has inspired staff to run the meetings again with current residents
- Funding was from Centrepoint's existing central funds

Contact

Jennie Blake
Life Skills and Youth Worker and co-ordinator of cooking project
Centrepoint Head Office
Central House
25 Camperdown Street
London E1 8DZ
Tel: 0845 466 3400
E-mail: jblake@centrepoint.org
Website: www.centrepoint.org.uk

Quotes

On young people hostels:
'We need more understanding of the population we are working with – we had no idea of who was here and how different their needs might be. The global education agenda needs to be part of our work. Youth work should be built in to hostel services.'

INCREASING UNDERSTANDING

9 Enfield Asylum Seekers Scrutiny Commission Panel, Enfield Council

The Project
The Enfield Asylum Seekers Scrutiny Commission was set up to establish the facts about asylum seekers in Enfield and dispel myths. Consisting of a panel of eight councillors from all three major political parties, it gathered evidence from local sources and presented its finding to a public meeting attended by asylum seekers, refugees and established residents.

Background
The London Borough of Enfield has a population of 280,000 and is the fifth most populated borough in London. More than 35 per cent are from ethnic minorities. The largest ethnic minority community in Enfield is Turkish.

Why do it?
The Enfield Asylum Seekers Scrutiny Commission was formed in response to concerns expressed by residents during the local election campaign in 2002.

Key Concerns
Locals
- Residents were concerned about the benefits they perceived asylum seekers to be receiving, relating to housing and public services
- Issues of overcrowding in the borough were also raised

Newcomers
- Access to services, including healthcare and training
- Wanting to make a valuable contribution to the borough

Approach and Activities
The Overview and Scrutiny Committee selects one issue to focus on per year. In 2002–3 the issue of asylum seekers was chosen.

The key activities of the Scrutiny Commission Panel included:

- two panel meetings in order to gather facts and information about matters relating to asylum seekers in Enfield;
- stakeholder consultation – included meetings with Refugee Community Organisations (RCOs), BME groups, the Refugee Council and local Primary Care Trusts;
- a public meeting held in May 2003 attended by approximately 100 people. Facts about asylum seekers were presented by the panel and the public were invited to ask questions in a similar format to the BBC's *Question Time* programme. The meeting covered several subjects including health, crime and housing;
- the findings from the meetings and consultations were summarised in a final report, accompanied by a fact sheet on asylum.

Aims
- To establish the facts about asylum seekers in Enfield and dispel any myths
- To raise levels of understanding in the local community

Achievements
- An issue that was of concern to local residents was addressed and dealt with in a structured format
- A secondary outcome was the production of an orientation guide for asylum seekers, produced in several languages and published in October 2004
- Overall a greater understanding of asylum seekers in Enfield was achieved by both residents and councillors alike
- Prior to the project, the local media published negative stories about asylum seekers; however as a result of the panel's work, both the *Enfield Advertiser* and *Enfield Independent* ran positive editorials following the public meeting
- The work has been recognised as a model of good practice across the country and other councils have requested copies of the final report to inform their future panels

How do we know?
- Complimentary letters were received from the community sector
- There have been fewer concerns voiced to councillors about asylum seekers in Enfield as a result of the panel's work

What Made a Difference?

Internal Factors
Cross-party co-operation between the councillors was a major strength. Councillors put their political interests aside and focused on the aims of the project.

External factors
Engaging asylum seekers was difficult. However, the panel did meet with representatives from the voluntary and community sector, including the Tamil Centre and Turkish support groups.

> **OPINION**
> *Enfield Gazette, Thursday May 15 2003*
>
> **Asylum-seekers provoke heated debate but rational conclusions are needed**
>
> **ENFIELD GAZETTE – ESTABLISHED 1859**
>
> THERE are certain similarities between events at Enfield Civic Centre and Broxbourne Council's offices in Cheshunt which both took place on Tuesday night.
>
> At the first venue, residents voiced their concern about refugees at the first public meeting of the council's asylum-seekers scrutiny commission.
>
> At the second, Broxbourne's first BNP member, Ramon Johns, appeared at his first council function against a backdrop of protests.
>
> But it is important that the facts do not get clouded by prejudice and distortion. The number of asylum seekers in Enfield is around 2,000 – or less than one per cent of the borough's population. The figure in Broxbourne is even lower.
>
> And, as the asylum-seekers scrutiny commission found, these asylum seekers do not receive preferential treatment when it comes to school places and health treatment, as urban myth dictates.
>
> There are many concerns about asylum-seekers, not least the cost incurred by the taxpayer for supporting them.
>
> But is important that these issues are sensibly and soberly debated, within both a local and national context.
>
> There are, naturally, exceptions, but the former chairman of the Enfield Racial Equality Council, Sam Bell, is surely right to say the majority of asylum-seekers are decent people.
>
> It is now up to the residents of Enfield and Broxbourne to show that they are decent people, too.

Published in the *Enfield Gazette* on May 15, 2003

Key Messages

- The whole spectrum of issues relating to asylum seekers in Enfield was considered, as opposed to one particular theme
- Most of all, the project focused on how the issue of asylum seekers affects local people and local services

Facts and Figures

- Local authority Scrutiny Commissions are cross-party bodies of councillors whose functions are, amongst others, to hold the executive to account, review and develop policy, review best value, engage partner organisations, the public and the press
- The fact sheet produced in May 2003 was re-run three times due to popular demand
- The Scrutiny Commission Panel reconvened in February 2004 to review the project and monitor the findings and recommendations
- All funding was secured from internal sources and council staff time was used

Contact

Mr Mike Ahuja
Lead Support Officer to the Scrutiny Commission
Enfield Council
Civic Centre
Silver Street
Enfield EN1 3XY
Tel: 020 8379 1000
E-mail: mike.ahuja@enfield.gov.uk
Website: www.enfield.gov.uk

Quotes

'We don't have a big outcry about asylum seekers now. It has taken some time but now it's being evidenced. The councillors deserve to take a bow for this. They did a lot to explode the myths and they continue to spread the word.'
Mike Ahuja

INCREASING UNDERSTANDING

10 Refugee Awareness Project, Refugee Action

The Project

Refugee Action's Refugee Awareness Project aims to reduce the climate of hostility that refugees and asylum seekers face by improving understanding of refugee and asylum issues amongst local communities.

The project is modelled on a pilot – the Volunteer Advocacy Project – which took place in Nottingham in 2002 and 2003. It has been included in this Handbook because of its strategic and national approach and because of its commitment to and tools for monitoring impact.

The project trains and supports refugees, asylum seekers and other local residents to run interactive awareness-raising sessions with key local community groups, from residents' associations and voluntary organisations to football teams and youth clubs.

The project encourages those who attend sessions to 'cascade' information to their colleagues, friends and neighbours, and supports groups in taking a proactive approach to welcoming refugees and asylum seekers in their area and involving them in community life.

Background

The project is running in three regions of England: the North West, South West and East Midlands.

Why do it?

The Refugee Awareness Project responds to Refugee Action's concern about national levels of misinformation on and hostility towards refugees and asylum seekers. These are manifested in incidences of racial harassment involving refugees, difficulties for refugees and asylum seekers in accessing services, the existence of local campaigns against refugees and asylum seekers and media coverage.

Approach and Activities

- Specially tailored awareness-raising presentations by refugees and established community volunteers to local groups and individuals, including information that challenges local myths about asylum and addresses specific concerns raised by attendees and real-life stories of refugees and asylum seekers who have settled in the UK
- Recruitment of volunteers from refugee and non-refugee backgrounds
- Training of volunteers in public speaking and facilitation skills and on the asylum system, host community concerns and public attitudes
- Development of materials and resources to be used by volunteers to deliver sessions
- Follow-up advice to groups so they can raise awareness locally and carry out practical initiatives to promote integration
- Marketing of the project
- Work with the local press in each area to promote positive stories of refugees

The approach is a combination of information provision and 'contact theory', where the host community are encouraged to meet and discuss issues with a refugee. The project does not set out to tell people what to think but aims instead to provide an interactive forum for balanced and informed discussion in which people can raise issues and be provided with honest answers by other local residents. The use of non-refugee volunteers drawn from local communities is key to this approach, which places importance on the attitudes of host communities, relations between host and refugee communities, and the empowerment and support of refugees.

The sessions are targeted at groups identified as key influencers in local communities. Examples are business and residents groups, parish councils, sports clubs, faith groups and organisations working with young people. By raising their awareness of asylum issues and providing follow-up support, it is hoped that these groups will then influence other residents.

Aims

Using a strategic and national approach, to inform local communities about asylum issues so that they become more welcoming to refugees and asylum seekers.

Achievements

It is early days for the project, but the pilot in Nottingham achieved:

- a positive change in the understanding of refugee and asylum issues by participants in sessions;
- all volunteers enjoyed being involved in the project, particularly because it gave them opportunities for personal development and to challenge negative images about refugees and asylum seekers;
- refugee and asylum-seeking volunteers felt that it gave them a voice.

How do we know?

- Audience response – short anonymous questionnaires at the beginning and end of each session, and semi-structured interviews with members of some groups several months later to assess longer-term impact
- Volunteer feedback – training feedback and exit questionnaires
- Local attitudes in areas where sessions are given – interviews with key local individuals
- Media coverage – media monitoring, particularly of letters to the editor
- Levels of fear amongst Refugee Action's clients, as well as degree of integration and sense of belonging – assessed through Refugee Action's biannual feedback survey
- Attacks – recorded in police and other agencies' racial incident monitoring reports and Refugee Action's biannual feedback survey
- Context – the creation of national and local timelines to log important incidents that might impact on the baseline of public opinion and affect take-up of the project

What Made a Difference?

- Enabling refugees and asylum seekers to talk to groups about their own experiences
- No refugee or asylum-seeking volunteer is required to speak about their personal experience if they do not wish to
- The use of both refugee and non-refugee presenters is key
- Making links with the organisations that the project wishes to target is time consuming; however once links are made with one organisation then quite often similar organisations will approach the project of their own accord
- The project design is heavily influenced by what was learnt from the pilot project and by an extensive literature review of research on public attitudes towards asylum, media and political images of asylum, and on asylum and community relations
- The project is firmly focused on awareness raising as opposed to training
- Volunteers are deliberately not recruited or marketed as 'experts' on asylum issues but as people who either originate from within the host community, and therefore understand its perspective, or people with a refugee background who understand this perspective
- A media strategy is in place, training volunteers to act as media spokespeople for the project

Key Messages

- Refugee Action's approach to refugee community development encompasses three elements: the attitudes of established communities, the empowerment and support of refugees, and relations between the two communities
- Refugee Action believes that the best way to promote understanding towards its clients is for people to meet a refugee or asylum seeker and hear their personal story
- It has been difficult to reach the groups Refugee Action most wanted to, some of which have hostile views. More engaging advertising materials are needed to gain the interest of and counter the initial fears of such groups

Facts and Figures

- The project aims to hold 750 awareness-raising sessions a year between 2005 and 2008
- The pilot in Nottingham delivered 59 presentations to an estimated 970 people in seven months
- A full-time project worker operates in each of the three regions
- 20 volunteers, half from refugee backgrounds, work in each of the three regions
- The project is funded by the Big Lottery Fund, the Calouste Gulbenkian Foundation, Lloyds TSB Foundations and the European Refugee Fund
- A similar but smaller scale project, the 1City Project, is being run in Peterborough. For more information on this, contact the Co-ordinator, Qamer Nissa, Tel: 01733 742812, E-mail: Qamer@menter.org.uk

Contact

Esme Peach
Communications Officer
Refugee Action
The Old Fire Station
150 Waterloo Road
London SE1 8SB
Tel: 020 7654 7700
E-mail: esmep@refugee-action.org.uk
Website: www.refugee-action.org.uk

Quotes

'When I tell people my story I often see a change in their attitude. When people hear the real facts about asylum they sometimes think again.'
Alain from Cameroon

'I thought it was fantastic the way actual young people seeking asylum gave us a brief history of themselves and I would like this to happen at our youth club in the future.'
Youth group worker

LOCAL INTEGRATION

11 Football Project, Asylum Seekers and Refugees of Kingston-upon-Hull

The Project
The project supports a group of mainly Kurdish refugees and asylum seekers to play football within established football leagues. Backed by a local voluntary group, Asylum Seekers and Refugees of Kingston-upon-Hull (ARKH), the project has sent teams to Kick It Out (anti-racism in football) events. More generally it also offers support, mentoring and advocacy.

Background
Kingston-upon-Hull is a dispersal area and there are currently around 1,500 asylum seekers housed by the National Asylum Support Service. The number of newcomers has increased in recent years: the local ethnic minority population in 2002 was 4 per cent compared to one per cent in 1996. This was largely due to the arrival of over 1,000 Iraqi Kurds between 1999 and 2000. The area has experienced problems at community level but attitudes have started to become more positive in the last two years.

Why do it?
The Spring Bank Tigers football team, and local asylum seekers and refugees in general, were facing significant local hostility and racism. A number of their matches had been affected by disturbances between rival players. Players from local teams racially abused Spring Bank players and there had been some retaliatory violence. The local Football Association (East Riding County FA) became involved and threatened to ban the team from the league. At this point the team turned to the ARKH for support.

Key Concerns
Locals
Refugees and asylum seekers are seen as a security threat, both as terrorists and as a danger to young local women.

Newcomers
- Not being accepted by local people
- Having qualifications overlooked by job centres
- Not knowing how to make complaints

Approach and Activities
Members of ARKH initially helped organise the team management committee, represented the team at league meetings and fundraised for strips. Now activities include:

- organising of training and matches;
- translation of rules into Kurdish;
- sending teams to new competitions such as the Unity Cup and the Kick It Out campaign.

The central approach is bringing people together through sport. The project tries to involve local people in everything it does, so that nothing is done only for refugees and asylum seekers. ARKH believes that sport can break down barriers between locals and newcomers.

The project started from the premise that the Spring Bank Tigers might have to behave better than other teams to be accepted. Direct contact outside of matches has been achieved through inviting other teams to their AGM. The project aims to enable team members to run and organise the team themselves.

Aims
- To get teams playing and being accepted in local leagues
- To encourage friendships across teams
- To inform host communities about the situation and life of refugees and asylum seekers

Achievements
- The first accepted asylum-seeker team in the area with its own AGM and constitution
- Improvement in the confidence and self-control of players
- Improvement in their English language skills
- Friendships formed with members of other teams, whose attitudes towards the team have changed

How do we know?
Anecdotal and observed evidence; no formal evaluation.

What Made a Difference?

Internal factors
- Laying initial ground rules and establishing a constitution
- Involving the players in the running and management of the team

External factors
The different cultural norms of English football in terms of rules and regulations.

Key Messages
- Much of the local population knows nothing of the Kurdish culture as the Kurds in this project knew little of the local culture in Hull
- Gaining acceptance and forging friendships with other teams is a slow process
- Funders need to be flexible over accountability

Facts and Figures
- The project formally began in summer 2004
- The team is funded by the Community Investment Fund and Hull Asylum Team
- ARKH provides premises, staff time, volunteers and advice
- Currently, the team has around 25–40 players regularly attending training and around 15 supporters who are also involved in the organisation of the team

Contact
Lynne Colley
ARKH
22–3 Albion St
Hull
East Yorkshire HU1 3TG
Tel: 01482 214178
E-mail: shna@arkh.hullresidents.net

Quotes
'A number of players from other teams came (to the AGM) and were treated to Kurdish dancing and food – culminating in 50 men drinking and dancing together!'

'Spring Bank players now feel comfortable going to watch a game in a pub, sharing jokes with locals over team allegiances.'

'I told the players that they have to behave better than everyone else. It might not be fair, but they are the newcomers and that is what they will have to do if they want to improve relations with other teams.'
Lynne Colley, ARKH

LOCAL INTEGRATION

12 Derwent Zambezi Association

The Project
Starting out as a small informal Refugee Community Organisation (RCO), the Derwent Zambezi Association (DZA) is now a constituted community organisation made up of refugees and asylum seekers and members drawn from the local host community, all of whom are volunteers. The refugee members are from different communities, unlike RCOs that traditionally represent a single population group. Based in the deprived, majority white working-class Derwent estate in Derby, the Association runs sport, choir and informal awareness-raising activities.

Background
A deprived area earmarked for investment under the government's New Deal for Communities (NDC) programme, Derwent, or Chaddesden as it is known locally, is a working-class neighbourhood of Derby, with a population of 10,000 in 4,200 households, of whom 98 per cent are white. It has a bad reputation locally and Asian taxi drivers are reported to be afraid of visiting the area. With dispersal, Normanton, the traditional black and minority ethnic (BME) area, was seen to be 'saturated' so families were placed in Derwent. Around 30 settled but fewer remain.

Why do it?
The new families were from many different countries and the community was fragmented with many feeling isolated. Racism and fear of racism was high. Bricks were thrown through the windows of newcomers, easily identifiable from the identical curtains given to them by the local authority.

Key Concerns
Locals
Asylum seekers received free decent furniture and benefits. This is a very deprived area and locals felt newcomers were unfairly accessing help and support at their expense.

Newcomers
Initially it was safety, not being able to live in peace. Now most recent arrivals are getting on and feel part of the community.

Approach and Activities
- A mixed choir of around 15 people learn songs and perform them in different languages both within and outside the area. The main aim is to bring people together particularly during choir practice
- A football club: Derwent FC started with an Under 14 side and now has four teams of different age groups, including an adult team. The players are drawn from both communities; the majority being established residents
- Awareness raising: one-off talks and presentations at local schools, church and agencies, and during refugee week, presented by refugee speakers on why they came to the UK, their culture and customs
- Social events including a party with African food and music at the local pub

The overall approach is bringing people together in shared leisure activities combined with some direct awareness raising. The organisation itself is inclusive in that its membership is a mix of new and established residents. The choir brings people together in a situation where all make an effort to learn songs in a different language. The football team brings people together in sport. Awareness raising helps teachers understand refugee children. An event at a local pub was organised to 'share culture and introduce people to us'. There were reported incidents of crime and aggressive behaviour at the pub and the landlord was worried about renting out the function room. Although regulars were initially suspicious, they were disarmed by the welcome, the offers of food and on seeing local people they recognised. Later some insisted on keeping African music on instead of UK pop.

Aims
To promote peaceful coexistence amongst community groups and build bridges between refugees and asylum seekers and the local host community.

Achievements
- It brought people together through football and singing
- Some asylum seekers and refugees have changed their minds about moving out of the area
- Host families have invited the children of newcomers to 'sleep over'
- Teachers have requested follow-up talks at the local school
- There has been anonymous gift-bringing at Christmas
- Asylum seekers and refugees feel more confident to express their culture, for example, through dancing at local events
- The choir has given performances outside the area and has contributed to a CD for World Song Music, which promotes grassroots talent
- The football team continues to expand with under 12, 14, 16 and adult teams, all of which are affiliated to the local Football Association

How do we know?
From informal feedback and anecdotal information from members.

What Made a Difference?
Internal factors
- An inclusive membership policy. It is believed that residents' negative attitudes towards newcomers, whom they perceived to be unfairly advantaged, would only have increased if the organisation had been set up for refugees and asylum seekers alone
- A sensitive, diplomatic and non-confrontational approach
- The commitment and perseverance of key individuals
- A small grant from the Office of the Deputy Prime Minister (ODPM)-funded NDC helped set up and sustain the project

External factors

While not negative in general the local press has more recently run positive features on the choir and the football team. It has also covered some deportation cases sympathetically.

Key Messages

- People change when personal relationships start to grow
- You need patience, tolerance and perseverance
- It is about achieving 'balance' and not 'forcing too much down people's throats' about asylum
- It is impossible to please everyone in this type of work
- It is a long process and it is unfinished
- It is important to involve everyone, especially children and their parents

Facts and Figures

- DZA was founded in 2003
- There are between 30 and 50 active members, all volunteers
- The management committee is made up of three refugees and asylum seekers, two established residents and one naturalised British citizen
- DZA has been helped by a small grant of under £10,000 through NDC and assisted by support from Refugee Action
- The work of DZA has been further assisted by First Steps, Living in Derwent, local schools, Derby World Song Music, Derby City Council Sports Development Office, Sporting Futures, Barclaycard and Derbyshire Community Foundation

Contact

Emilio Tavares
Chair
Derwent Zambezi Association
16 St Marks Road
Derwent
Derby DE21 4AH
Tel: 01332 378866
E-mail: emilio.tavares@derby.gov.uk

Quotes

'I asked myself do I stay or do I go [leave the area]? If I stay, do I just sit here and say "they are all racists?" Or do I do something? We've all got the same issues. This area is "ours". We all want to restore pride and fight the bad reputation of Chaddesden.'

'You can't be angry when you sing, only peaceful.'

'The football is about playing football. If you had a talk on race relations you might provoke trouble. Fights will be about football, not other things.'

'It all boils down to personal relationships. You must personalise it, otherwise it's just dreams and theory.'
Emilio Tavares, DZA Chair

LOCAL INTEGRATION

13 Derwent Refugee Community Development Support Project, Refugee Action

The Project
The project provides drop-in advice and assistance on a one-to-one basis. A resource room is also available with the use of a PC, fax and telephone. The project is engaged in awareness raising which has involved a series of myth-busting and question and answer sessions with refugee speakers. There have been one-off events such as a carnival and presentations in schools. In conjunction with Timebank there is a 'buddying project' which pairs up refugees and asylum seekers with members of the host community. The project has also set up a racial harassment steering group which aims to engage agencies with an interest in community safety and encourages action when an incident is reported.

Background
The project is located in a house on an estate in Derwent which is a neighbourhood of Derby. It is a white working-class area and there is a poor history of minority integration. Currently, 20 refugee and asylum-seeking families live in the area.

Why do it?
The Derwent neighbourhood has been identified as an area of high deprivation under the New Deal for Communities (NDC) programme. NDC approached Refugee Action because of the harassment and tension in the area since the dispersal of asylum seekers to Derwent.

Key Concerns

Locals
- 'Invasion'
- Fear of the unknown
- Unfair distribution of resources in favour of refugees and asylum seekers

Newcomers
At first there were fears around safety but now the majority are getting on with local residents.

Approach and Activities
In the initial stages of the project leaders introduced themselves to other NDC projects. They also knocked on the doors of refugees, asylum seekers and the host community and explained that people could attend their office for advice, a chat or for a cup of tea. Refugee Action joined in with existing activities, such as those organised by Timebank, and gave informal presentations. Local people were trained and empowered to deliver the work.

Aims
- To assist in the integration of refugee and asylum-seeking families on the estate
- To foster a more welcoming atmosphere
- To raise awareness amongst local people of asylum and refugee issues
- To improve access to services in the area
- To encourage refugees and asylum seekers to access NDC projects

Achievements
- A reduction in racial harassment incidents
- A greater understanding amongst members of the host community about refugees and asylum seekers and why they come to the UK
- The provision of a safe place for refugees and asylum seekers where they can be understood
- Co-ordination with other NDC projects on inclusion issues

How do we know?
- An external evaluation of the project has been carried out
- Outcomes were also informed by anecdotal evidence and self-evaluation

What Made a Difference?

Internal factors
- All the staff had good interpersonal skills and were able to communicate with all sections of the community
- The link worker is local and her family have a positive reputation in the area
- The choice of location for the project was important: when the office was moved to a more accessible part of the estate the service improved

External factors
The inclusion in wider NDC activities and strategy.

Key Messages
- If local people are trained and empowered to deliver the work then other local people are more likely to participate in the initiatives
- It is important to keep the project focused and not try to take on too much
- Related agencies need to be engaged from the beginning
- Funders need to be kept up to date with developments
- A steering group of local people ensures that feedback from the community is heard
- It is important to recognise that refugees, asylum seekers and the host community sometimes have the same needs
- Individuals need to be encouraged to take part for the first time and after that they are more likely to participate in other activities

Facts and Figures

- The NDC funded this project over three years
- 358 individuals have accessed awareness-raising training over the course of the project
- 400 copies of the project leaflet were distributed

Contact

Gail Pringle
Project Manager
Refugee Action
17 St Marks Road
Derwent
Derby DE21 6AH
Tel: 01332 361189
E-mail: gailp@refugee-action.org.uk
Website: www.refugee-action.org.uk

Quotes

'Placing people together when they are enjoying themselves and have a common aim is just as important as a formal awareness-raising event. Many people would run a mile if they see the word 'refugee' but would happily come to a football match or a barbeque.'
Gail Pringle

LOCAL INTEGRATION

14 Greater Pollock Settlement and Integration Network

The Project
The Greater Pollock Settlement and Integration Network (GPSIN) is one of ten city-wide networks set up between 2000 and 2002 to co-ordinate local responses to the needs of asylum seekers in Glasgow after the implementation of dispersal, and specifically to create a structure for the involvement of the voluntary sector in this process. The networks are area-based multi-agency partnerships which facilitate joint working across the statutory and voluntary sectors, while also encouraging community involvement.

Background
Around 12,500 asylum seekers have arrived in Glasgow since 2000, representing a 60 per cent increase in the black and minority ethnic (BME) population in the city. The resettlement process has been housing led, and asylum seekers have been dispersed to areas of housing surplus, primarily in areas of social deprivation. The population of Pollock is around 38,000 with the established BME population around 3 per cent and about 300 refugees and asylum seekers. Irish, Indian and Pakistani people have been the largest immigrant groups in recent decades and there is a new and growing Polish community of around 30 families.

Why do it?
When asylum-seeking families were first placed in Pollock, there was no structure or forum for the voluntary sector to address their needs here or anywhere else in the city. Glasgow City Council needed partners to help with their arrival and settlement and, with assistance from the Scottish Refugee Council and Glasgow Council for the Voluntary Sector, the City Council set up ten networks across the city. In Pollock the existing services were not close to where the newcomers lived. GPSIN's work has been reactive, responding to need.

Key Concerns
Locals
- Refugees and asylum seekers get better housing
- Refugees and asylum seekers do not want to work and are burdening health services

Newcomers
- Securing residency status, housing and employment and making friends
- Racism is also an issue and there has been some backlash from the July 2005 London bombings

Approach and Activities
- A Community Café drop-in, near where most new families are housed, runs a programme of social events and talks by local service providers
- Multicultural evenings led by partners, including one storytelling event attended by over 100 people from both established and new communities which led to two books being published
- A Food for Thought event with food from all over the world, including Scotland

- Sporting activities sponsored by the Healthy Living Initiative, including a one-off event involving 60–70 people and a football league involving the police, established residents and asylum seekers and refugees
- Involvement in wider activities such as the Pollock Games led by the Healthy Living Initiative which showcased traditional games from both communities and was attended by 2000 people
- Social events with other networks, including the Pollokshaw Festival, a multicultural celebratory event with major participation from the local community
- Awareness raising in schools with Strathclyde Police
- An information leaflet tackling myths about refugees and asylum seekers, which was subsequently adapted and used by other networks
- Monthly meetings to review and plan work
- Annual development day for partners and potential new partners to review work and get commitment for future work

The overall approach is the organisation of shared social activities, the assumption being that common interests bring people together.

Using a multi-agency approach, GPSIN either organises or participates in local social and sports events, supporting this with awareness-raising information disseminated through fact sheets and sessions at schools. The emphasis is on ownership from within the community and enabling refugee and asylum-seeking residents to do community engagement work. The Community Café provides a space for people to meet and a hub where local providers run health promotion activities, emergency services presentations and similar events. Awareness raising in local schools involves representatives from the network, including refugees, teaming up with the police on their crime and safety visits and running question and answer sessions on the backgrounds and real-life experiences of asylum seekers and refugees. The network liaises with the local media to publicise its work.

Aims

To promote integration between asylum seekers and host communities through a range of initiatives and specifically to:

- engage key local individuals and organisations from all sectors in planning around asylum and integration issues;
- act as an advocating body for, and spread positives messages about, refugees and asylum seekers in host communities;
- share information about issues and concerns affecting refugees and asylum seekers and the local host community.

Achievements

- The bringing together of different agencies around one table to respond to issues raised by refugees and asylum seekers

- With leadership from the Healthy Living Initiative and the police, the Community Café has successfully brought new and established residents together. A new 'fruit barra' will sell fresh fruit at cost price and further draw people in
- GPSIN believes that refugees and asylum seekers have successfully settled into the community and now feel safe and supported in the area. Individual newcomers are beginning to stand up and speak at public events
- It has been very effective in getting asylum seekers involved in local social events designed as a forum for asylum-seeking and host communities to meet
- A highly successful summer arts and music programme culminating in the Big Day Out in Pollock, an event including a ceilidh and activities involving asylum seekers' own national dress and dance, was praised as an excellent way of initiating friendships

How do we know?

- From an external review of the ten networks in Glasgow by the Scottish Centre for Research on Social Justice, *Building Bridges: Local responses to the resettlement of asylum seekers on Glasgow* (October 2004)
- Evaluation sheets put out for every event
- Personal observations and anecdotes
- People coming back to the Café where comments and feedback are written on a 'Talking Wall'. After one event, one person wrote: 'For the first time for a long time I felt at home.'
- It is becoming easier to find places to put on refugee and asylum seeker events

What Made a Difference?

Internal factors

- The commitment shown by partners, some of whom give up their weekends to attend events
- Involving people with influence at policy levels, such as local councillors
- Giving refugees and asylum seekers the opportunity to do community work; GPSIN's chair is a refugee from the area
- Putting serious messages across in a safe, friendly environment
- Reaching the wider established community has not been easy; however, football was one way of engaging 'harder-to-reach' people

External factors

- The Scottish Executive's integration strategy is to ensure that the needs of newcomers are met within the structures of mainstream service provision for the wider community rather than promoting separate specialist service provision
- The local *Pollock Post* is community-led and positive
- Some agencies are seen to be resistant to change, especially within the statutory sector which is used to seeking quantifiable evidence for success rather than 'soft' outcomes

Key Messages
- Keep targets fluid; needs change and you have to change with them
- Relationships need time to develop; it is important not to put false deadlines on things
- Skills are more important than resources for taking things forward
- Patience and commitment are essential
- This work cannot be done in isolation; partners are crucial
- Administrative support is very important; having someone who can take minutes and organise meetings
- Keep key people such as local councillors and members of the Scottish Executive on board so messages go back to policymakers
- Engage media at a local level because this is where impact is aimed

Facts and Figures
- GPSIN's active partners include: Greater Pollock Healthy Living Initiative, Glasgow Asylum Support Project, Greater Pollock Social Inclusion Partnership, YMCA, Citizens Advice Bureau, local colleges, Scottish Refugee Council, Glasgow City Council Cultural and Leisure Services, local churches, Village Project
- GPSIN's work is managed by the partners, with the Greater Pollock Healthy Living Initiative taking a lead role. It is administered by the City Council social work team
- GPSIN is funded by the Scottish Executive through the local Social Inclusion Partnership
- Each of the ten Glasgow integration networks sends a representative to the Community Responses Co-ordinating Group which enables local networks to raise issues of concern at a city-wide, strategic level
- GPSIN is part of a Glasgow-wide initiative to build dialogue between refugee and host communities and agencies. Run by the Scottish Refugee Council, the 'Framework for Dialogue' has held large consultation events with asylum seekers and local community leaders across the city since 2002, aimed at ensuring refugee participation in planning local services and longer-term integration between new and existing communities. For more details contact Mick Doyle on Tel: 0141 248 9799, E-mail Mick.Doyle@scottishrefugeecouncil.org.uk.

Contact
Beltus Etchu
Chair of GPSIN
or Linda McGlynn
Greater Pollock Healthy Living Initiative
31 Corkerhill Place
Corkerhill
Pollock G52 1RU
Tel: 0141 892 0638
E-mail: etchu77@yahoo.co.uk or Linda.McGlynn@gphli.org.uk

Information also provided by: George Daly, network member.

Quotes

'You have to bring people together through what they enjoy doing.'

'I am from the community. If you don't get involved no one will listen to you. If you stay in isolation nothing will happen.'

'A woman stopped me in the street on the way here and said "You spoke in my daughter's school." She invited me in for a cup of tea and told me her attitude [towards asylum seekers] had changed.'
Beltus Etchu, Chair of the Greater Pollock Settlement and Integration Network

'We are starting to reach the wider community but there's still a long way to go. The work is ongoing.'

'Everything we do is about respect and understanding and where the similarities are.'
George Daly, network member and chair of the Greater Pollock Healthy Living Initiative

LOCAL INTEGRATION

15 Swansea Bay Asylum Seekers Support Group

The Project
The main focus of the project is a bi-weekly drop-in session, which provides a play group, legal advice, an information service and mentoring in partnership with other organisations. The project also organises courses, social and cultural events, anti-deportation campaigns and public education meetings and initiatives.

Background
The project is based in Swansea which has a population of 200,000. There are around 1,000 asylum seekers and the project estimates a 'few hundred' refugees living in the city. The largest newcomer groups are Pakistanis, Kurds, Iranians and Francophone Africans. The existing ethnic minority population is small and consists mainly of Bangladeshis and Chinese, so the recent arrival of refugees and asylum seekers has made quite a visible difference in some areas. New arrivals are placed on estates with high levels of social deprivation where experiences range from 'harassment to adoption by local families'.

Why do it?
Various groups had identified problems of poverty and hardship amongst refugees and asylum seekers living in Swansea. Existing forms of service provision for this group were inadequate and the project leaders saw a need for a space where refugees and asylum seekers could meet and obtain advice on a regular basis. They also identified a need for public education on refugee and asylum issues.

Key Concerns

Locals
There is a general climate of tolerance but also concerns around competition for resources.

Newcomers
Have fears regarding the safety of living in certain areas of the city.

Approach and Activities
- A welcome party for early arrivals of asylum seekers hosted by the mayor
- A drop-in centre for asylum seekers and refugees offering general and legal advice from partners, and support
- One-to-one mentoring between host community volunteers and newcomers
- Public meetings to present factual information about asylum
- Social events such as a summer barbeque, a kids' Christmas party

- A football team
- Dissemination of three books showcasing local and refugee writers

The general approach is to organise joint social activities backed up by public presentation of 'myth-busting' information about asylum seekers and refugees. Project leaders aim to create opportunities for people from different groups to mix and 'let them get on with it'. The social events are attended by the whole community. Refugees and asylum seekers are encouraged to bring their neighbours and a number of people from the host community attend. When the asylum dispersal policy was first announced the group produced a newsletter entitled *Refugees are Welcome Here* and handed it out in the town shopping centre. Most activities are led by the volunteers, who come from the refugee and asylum-seeker community as well as the host community.

Aims

- To provide assistance for refugees and asylum seekers, improve their living conditions and include them in decision-making about local services
- To raise awareness amongst the host community about this group
- To build our capacity as a community of locals, asylum seekers and refugees working together

Achievements

- More than 70 people attended a recent public meeting which used refugee speakers to present 'myth-busting' information about asylum seekers and refugees
- The project has become a symbol of bridge-building
- Demonstrated to local residents what the local host community can do
- Successfully engaged local public figures, such as the mayor

How do we know?
- Observations of project leaders
- No formal evaluation

What Made a Difference?

Internal factors
- All of the staff at the project are volunteers
- The availability of a free venue for the drop-in sessions
- Active involvement of partner agencies
- Good relations with the local press

Key Messages

The commitment of unpaid volunteers, their willingness, time and trust are key.

Facts and Figures
- There is no core funding. Most activities are run on a voluntary basis. Small pots of money have been provided for individual projects
- Half the volunteers are from the established community and half are refugees or asylum seekers
- Partner agencies include Supporting Others through Volunteer Action (SOVA), Asylum Justice and University of Wales Adult Education Department

Contact
Tom Cheesman
Activities Organiser and Treasurer
c/o The Retreat
2 Humphrey Street
Swansea SA1 6BG
E-mail: t.cheesman@swan.ac.uk

Quotes
'We were all very apprehensive when we knew that an asylum seeker was coming to live amongst us, but we had no need to worry, she has been a joy to live next door to… We hope that Adan and the children can stay and that this letter will help her realise her dream of staying and belonging.'
Extract from a letter of support published in the Swansea Bay Asylum Seekers Support Group's book, *Nobody's Perfect*

LOCAL INTEGRATION

16 Victoria Estate Action Group

The Project
The Victoria Estate Action Group (VEAG) was established in 1990 by a small group of elderly local residents who were exasperated with their estate's problems and the perceived lack of attention from the council. In 1994 the group moved into an unoccupied house on the edge of the estate and opened it as a place for local people to use as a community space for meetings and activities. The building is open all day during the week and the council, local advice services, debt agencies and drug and alcohol support groups hold regular sessions there.

Background
The Victoria Estate, close to Stockton-on-Tees town centre, comprises 420 households. Until the late 1970s this was considered a popular place to live, close to local amenities and places of work, with a stable population living in the estate's flats and maisonettes. But in the 1980s, when the North East was hit hard by the decline of local industries, levels of unemployment and crime increased and the estate began to empty as those that could afford to move, did. Though there is a small ethnic minority population, the majority of the community is white. Twenty-three new asylum-seeking families have recently moved into the estate.

Why do it?
In the last three to four years asylum seekers have been moved into the empty flats on the Victoria Estate. The VEAG became concerned about violence towards asylum seekers and were keen to prevent this happening. The Council now informs the group when newcomers are moved onto the estate so that they can be welcomed and introduced to their neighbours. Asylum seekers given leave to remain in the UK encountered problems receiving immediate benefits and many in the area were destitute; the project was also set up as a response to this.

Key Concerns

Locals
Residents thought asylum seekers were being given brand new furniture and generous benefits when they first moved in. The common view was, 'We've lived here all our lives and never got given anything like this.' Others were simply curious as they had had little contact with people from other countries.

Newcomers
The experience of this project suggests that newcomers kept their concerns to themselves and did not complain as they were principally interested in getting themselves 'on their feet quickly'.

Approach and Activities
- Welcome and introduction: local tenants' officers introduce new residents to the VEAG house when they move in. The group offers them an introduction to the area, helps them settle in and provides whatever other assistance they can
- The project operates a laundry service for asylum seekers and distributes donated clothes and furniture to people who arrive with nothing

- The group disseminates information on asylum seeker and refugee entitlements to local households verbally and through newsletters
- Informal English classes are run by other agencies who rent space at the house, available to all residents

The local residents group proactively welcomes newcomers to the area, offers a joint resource and acts as 'brokers' with other residents. The group has involved established residents in helping newcomers move in 'so they could see for themselves what they had [and] tell others the situation'. When new families began to arrive, group members asked the Council for information on benefits they were receiving. This information was then circulated among other residents, by knocking on doors and posting newsletters. The VEAG house is a resource for everyone on the estate, which newcomers and established residents alike use for socialising and for its services and facilities.

Aims
- To improve the quality of life on the estate
- To enable all local residents to live in harmony with each other
- To reduce isolation for vulnerable people
- To build a more united community

Achievements
- Both established and new residents have learned about each other
- New friendships have been made
- Race is rarely a factor in resident complaints

How do we know?
From informal feedback from residents and general observations from group members.

What Made a Difference?
Internal factors
The commitment of the members, all of whom are volunteers.

Key Messages
- 'Don't go into these things half-heartedly. It's no good starting to be someone's friend and then disappearing'
- This kind of project requires dedication

Facts and Figures
- The VEAG is led and managed by a group of eight volunteers, all elderly, who live on the estate
- On average about 30 residents a day drop in to the house for advice, to socialise or to attend a course

- Collaborating agencies include: the local authority, Tristar housing management company, the police, and Stockton Residents Group
- Expenses are funded through charging for room hire in the building
- Advice and courses at the house are funded and run by external agencies

Contact

Vera Walker
VEAG volunteer manager
Victoria Estate Action Group
9 Cromwell Avenue
Stockton-On-Tees
Cleveland TS18 2EF
Tel: 01642 670670

Quotes

'There was a lack of preparation for people moving into the area, which caused a lot of misunderstanding. People should have been paid to make proper arrangements for the newcomers. Locals should have been informed and consulted. No one came and told us what was happening.'

'We don't see it as a project ... there's no design just common sense. If they are coming to live in our communities let's all be friends and learn from each other and treat them the same as we want to be treated.'

'When a house becomes vacant, you hear many people now saying "see if you can get a refugee [to live in it]".'
Vera Walker

PERSONAL DEVELOPMENT

17 The Bridges Project

The Project
The Bridges Project is the only work experience scheme for asylum seekers and refugees in Scotland. Work shadowing is a tried and tested way for individuals to observe the work of others and gain first-hand experience of a working environment. The project places individuals on 12-week, one-day-a-week training programmes with local businesses.

Background
Glasgow is the largest dispersal region outside of London and the ethnic minority population of Glasgow was 7 per cent at the last census, but is likely to be higher now. About 12,500 asylum seekers have been dispersed to Glasgow in the last five years.

Why do it?
It is generally acknowledged that refugees and asylum seekers have under-utilised skills and that refugees can struggle to find employment. As there is little integration work beyond community settings, the project focuses on integrating people in the work place and sees this as a direct way of building bridges between refugees and asylum seekers and host communities as well as providing effective training.

Key Concerns
Locals
- One pharmaceutical shop feared adverse reactions from locals if it employed an asylum seeker
- Construction workers of one company held the opinion that asylum seekers did not want to work

Newcomers
- Difficulty in utilising previously learned skills
- Lack of understanding of employment regulations and work culture in the UK
- Asylum seekers are ineligible for paid employment

Approach and Activities
- Work placements and shadowing
- Assistance with CV writing, applications and interview preparation
- Referral for careers guidance and ESOL classes

This project enables newcomers and locals to be brought together in a real-life situation. Individuals participating in the scheme mainly focus on the work of one employee but they are also in daily contact with a range of other staff. New companies are inducted on asylum-seeker employment rights and responsibilities. The scheme is promoted at local colleges and community centres. Participants are assessed for educational background, work experience, skills and personal circumstances. They are then matched with a relevant business and assigned an appropriate role. Continued support is offered in the form of a personal development plan, one-to-one advice and case work. Placements are monitored and evaluated as they progress, with feedback from the client and the employer.

Aims
- To begin the economic integration of refugees as early as possible
- To develop and maintain the skills of refugees and asylum seekers in order to improve employability
- To improve the confidence of refugees and asylum seekers
- To benefit local employers

Achievements
- Improved employment opportunities
- Raised awareness amongst employers and individual employees
- Increased confidence among refugees and asylum seekers
- Enabled asylum seekers and refugees to have knowledge of local working culture

How do we know?
- Seven refugees have secured paid employment
- Positive feedback from employers and employees
- Recommended as a European model of good practice by an external evaluator

What Made a Difference?
Internal factors
- The project leader is a former journalist and has developed good media contacts which has resulted in positive publicity
- The project has a refugee steering group which helps develop services to meet the needs of the client group

External factors
- The local media in Glasgow has generally been very positive and a number of newspapers have taken people on placements. Two BBC Scotland documentaries have featured the project
- The city, and Scotland more generally, has a number of initiatives to attract foreign labour. This project is working within a wider strategy called Fresh Talent, an initiative of the Scottish Executive
- It is a constant challenge to attract new business sectors to the scheme

Key Messages
- Funders need to recognise that this type of project is a slow process
- Working in partnership is essential as there is a limit to what can be done alone
- Providing natural, real-life situations for local people to interact with refugees and asylum seekers is crucial for building bridges

Facts and Figures
- The project is funded by Equal (European Social Fund), the Scottish Executive, Children in Need, the Home Office and other small charitable trusts
- The scheme has been running since 2003
- Around 200 asylum seekers and refugees have been on work placements since the project's inception. Currently around 15 are being placed per month

Contact
Maggie Lennon
Project Director
Bridges Programmes
27 Main Street
Bridgeton, Glasgow G40 1QA
Tel: 0141 554 5440
E-mail: admin@bridgesprogrammes.org.uk
Website: www.bridgesprogrammes.org.uk

Quotes
'Building workers from one particular company had preconceived ideas about asylum seekers being scroungers and claiming benefits. Working with individual asylum seekers on placement they were surprised to find that asylum seekers are not allowed to work and faced other hardships. Personal contact made them change their views.'
Maggie Lennon, Project Director

'The bridges project does exactly what it is titled, bridging the gap between the society at large and asylum seekers… The scheme understands learning as a two-way process which is vital to the growth of any society.'
An employer

PERSONAL DEVELOPMENT

18 Learning to Advise, Stoke Citizens Advice Bureau

The Project
Learning to Advise is a training project which enables asylum seekers to become volunteer Citizens Advice Bureau (CAB) advisers.

Background
Stoke-on-Trent is an asylum dispersal town. Stoke CAB is one of the largest bureaux in the country and leads others on refugee/asylum issues and on training in general. It has 96 paid staff and 70–80 volunteers. It is the only advice service in Stoke open to everyone and offers a city-wide service.

Why do it?
Stoke CAB workforce consists of about 50 per cent volunteers who undergo a three-month training course. The CAB has a policy of trying to ensure that the staff and volunteer team is representative of the local communities who use the advice service. The project reflects this policy.

Asylum seekers were first dispersed to Stoke in 2000 and because there is no refugee agency in the town, they began to use the CAB for advice and so it set up an asylum-seekers team. The CAB also wished to have asylum seekers represented on its volunteer team. Several asylum seekers who had used the service also wanted to give something back by becoming advisers. However when some of them tried, they were unable to complete the training course due to a lack of understanding of the local community and customs and how the British welfare and legal systems worked.

Key Concerns
Newcomers
- Lack of knowledge of the British welfare and legal systems
- Concerns about local perceptions and misinformation spread by the media and politicians

Approach and Activities
Provision of a four-week (two half days and one full day per week) specially tailored access course for asylum-seeking volunteers, including:

- briefings on local history and the geographical communities of Stoke and a guided tour of the town;
- briefings on the welfare state and how it works locally;
- confidence and team-building work;
- briefings from providers of other services;
- additional support from the project worker during the training course.

In addition to the project some of the volunteers have given awareness-raising talks for the bureau in schools.

The project has not been set up specifically to meet the needs of asylum seekers, but to enable them to join in mainstream activities. It allows asylum seekers to be the ones doing the helping rather than being those in need of help, shifting the role of asylum seekers from client to colleague. When the groups mix for the first time the approach is relaxed and non-direct. Many of the host community volunteers have special needs and so the approach is one of valuing difference. Training involves group work and team building and is designed to get the group talking to and working together. Emphasis is placed on what unites the group as opposed to what divides them.

Aims

- To provide asylum seekers with the opportunity to gain training and improve employability
- To provide the bureau with a new group of volunteers enabling the team to represent service users more accurately
- To promote community cohesion by enabling interaction between asylum seekers and local community members

Achievements

- Provided recognised accreditation for participants
- Improved English language skills
- Increased confidence of participants in communicating and building relationships in various social settings
- Challenged the stereotypes that existing staff and non-asylum-seeking clients may have had

What Made a Difference?

Internal factors

- The project ultimately enabled asylum seekers to engage with local CAB clients for a purpose beyond trying to bring communities together
- The existing culture at the CAB is considered very inclusive and there was support from staff within the bureau who were not part of the project

Key Messages

Training asylum seekers, who are prohibited from paid employment, to provide a service as a volunteer enables them to be the helper, removing the perception of dependence.

Facts and Figures

- Around 10–15 per cent of total enquiries at Stoke CAB are from asylum seekers or refugees
- In the first year the project recruited three groups of ten volunteers
- Drop-out rates for asylum-seeker volunteers was lower (12 per cent) than the overall rate (33–50 per cent)
- Trainees receive certificates from the Open College Network and the Millennium Volunteer project

Contact

Jude Hawes
Project Manager
Stoke-on-Trent CAB
Advice House
Cheapside
Hanley
Stoke-on-Trent ST1 1HL
Tel: 01782 201234
E-mail: hawes@stoke-cab.org.uk
Website: www.stoke-cab.org.uk

Information also provided by: Jutta Möhrke, Project Worker.

Quotes

'Staff and volunteers have mentioned that they have challenged the attitudes of family and friends as a result of the project.'
Jude Hawes

'Before I didn't know anything about the British system or lifestyle… now I am really involved in the system with this training… I became close to the people in the community.'

'It helped me to forget that I am an asylum seeker…put me in a normal position…it developed my experience… especially if I meet local residents. I can tell them something that they don't understand.'
From participants in the project

PERSONAL DEVELOPMENT

19 Stress Leaflet Project, Mothertongue

The Project
The project was set-up by Mothertongue, a multi-ethnic counselling service, and involved young volunteers aged 14–19 years from local host and asylum-seeking communities in the creation of a stress management leaflet. The leaflet was produced in six languages: Albanian, Arabic, English, Farsi, French and Swahili. The volunteers organised the entire production of the leaflet, from interviewing young asylum seekers and researching the content of the leaflet, to designing and commissioning the final version.

Background
The project was based in the Abbey area of south-east Reading, where 81 per cent of residents are white British.

Why do it?
The project was established to alleviate the stress and mental health problems of young asylum seekers in the area. Local groups, health visitors, social workers and the local college raised concerns that there was a lack of written information for newly arrived young asylum seekers in their own languages. The project also sought to engage young asylum seekers and local young people and to give them skills in design and project management.

Key Concerns
Newcomers
- Immigration status, access to housing, employment issues and being able to learn English quickly
- Not being aware of all the services available to them in the area

Approach and Activities
- Recruitment of the young host community volunteers through the Anderson Baptist Church and their previous work with Supporting Asylum Seekers in Reading (SASIR)
- Recruitment of young asylum seekers through Reading College ESOL Department and the Reading Refugee Support Group
- The volunteers participated in a steering group which met once a month and discussed the design, content, cultural input and proposed distribution of the leaflet
- Interviewing young asylum seekers to find out what they needed from the leaflet and identifying the most commonly used languages
- Writing and designing the leaflet and translating the content into six languages
- Presenting the final product at a launch event

Aims
- To produce a leaflet in relevant languages, providing information to help young asylum seekers understand the causes of stress and learn ways to relieve it
- To promote understanding between asylum seekers and local young people
- To enable host community members and young asylum seekers to work together creatively and learn useful skills

Achievements

- The project raised awareness and promoted understanding between young local residents and young asylum seekers
- Project staff learnt about communicating with people from different cultures
- Volunteers developed skills, including in teamwork, writing proposals and budgets, interviewing techniques, design work and commissioning a printer
- Wide distribution of the leaflet

How do we know?
- Feedback forms were used at the launch event
- The project team carried out an evaluation exercise with the volunteers

What Made a Difference?

Internal factors

The young asylum seekers often faced practical problems, but still gave their time and energy to the project.

Key Messages

- Communicating with and learning from each other was the central ethos of the project
- A common activity provides a focus

Facts and Figures

- Mothertongue ran the project in collaboration with Anderson Youth and Scout Group, Anderson Baptist Church and SASIR
- 40–50 people were involved in the project
- The project was funded by Reading Primary Care Trust and Reading Borough Council

Contact

Beverley Costa
Project Manager
Mothertongue
PO Box 2409
Reading RG1 1ZQ
Tel: 0118 901 5749
E-mail: beverley@mothertongue.clara.co.uk
Website: www.mothertongue.org.uk

Quotes

'It made me laugh when my counsellor tried to say some of the words in my language and that is when I started to feel at ease with her.'
Client using the leaflet

PERSONAL DEVELOPMENT

20 Shared Road, Prince's Trust

The Project
Delivered by Prince's Trust Scotland, Shared Road works in partnership with the police, schools and city council to bring together young people aged 14–25 from refugee/asylum and local established communities living in the Red Road neighbourhood of north Glasgow. It provides a regular youth club with arts and sports activities ranging from DJing and body art to film-making and outdoor pursuits.

Background
Glasgow is the biggest dispersal region outside London, with 12,500 asylum seekers placed there in the last five years. The most recent census showed a 7 per cent BME population. The Red Road area of north Glasgow is dotted with 30-floor blocks of flats and experiences high levels of deprivation. Refugees and asylum seekers now make up over 10 per cent of the population. Twenty seven different languages are spoken at the local All Saints secondary school.

Why do it?
There has been tension between established locals and newcomers, including the murder of an asylum seeker on the nearby Sighthill estate in 2002 and the murder of a man in Glasgow city centre by a refugee in 2004. Generally, communities were not mixing. Asylum seekers were afraid to leave their homes at night and the police were increasingly concerned about youth conflict.

Key Concerns

Locals
That the asylum seekers and refugees arriving in the city do not want to work and are 'feeding off the state'.

Newcomers
- Uncertainty about their future
- Fear of deportation

Approach and Activities
A monthly evening event attracts around 70 young people to try out taster activities. In the early stages, when some young refugee and asylum seekers were afraid to go out after dark, the project arranged minibuses to and from the venue. The club is relaxed and informal, allowing participants to dip in and out of activities as they choose. The club also breaks off into smaller special interest groups of 10–15 where participants learn specialist skills and run a project together, meeting weekly.

The main approach is involving the two groups of young people in shared activities aimed at personal development and empowerment. The first step in this is removing fear, then creating a safe and relaxed environment, engaging participants, focusing on individual need and development and from there allowing friendships to occur naturally. The groups are small enough to enable youth workers to concentrate on personal development, yet large enough to encourage mixing and friendships. The club is led by a youth council ensuring that the project is user-directed.

Aims
- To combat racism and hostility
- To reduce youth disorder
- To tackle isolation and exclusion
- To create friendships

Achievements
- New friendships have been formed between groups
- Intolerance between different members of the community has been significantly lessened, with police reporting a reduction of local tensions
- The provision of a safe space for socialisation and interaction
- Participation in the 2005 World Youth Congress

How do we know this?
These outcomes were identified through a self-evaluation report and a central monitoring database.

What Made a Difference?

Internal factors
- Ownership of the project by participants
- A careful choice of venues with a relaxed environment
- Ensuring safety and reassuring cautious parents, including through providing transport to events
- Getting the right staff who can engage young people
- Using a school catchment area attracts people from the same community who may already know each other
- Heavy input at the start of the project such as promotion at the local school and knocking on people's doors got it off the ground
- Individuals are profiled and progress monitored on a central database
- Active engagement of local partners: promotion and assistance by the local school, police and local authority street youth teams

External factors
- A key difference between Glasgow and some of the cities in England is that Glasgow and Scotland genuinely want to attract and encourage immigration
- Local and national media reporting is now much more positive about refugees and asylum seekers and raises awareness of the conditions they face

Key Messages

Change does not happen overnight. It takes perseverance and a long-term commitment by staff and funders alike.

Facts and Figures

- 126 young people are registered with the project
- Membership is 50/50 local people/refugees and asylum seekers
- On a day-to-day basis the project is run by one full-time project manager, 15 sessional staff and volunteers
- Key working partners: All Saints School, the local police force, SpiritAid, Impact Arts, North Glasgow College, Media Co-op, Gary Mitchell song and dance performance group
- Funded by the Home Office Challenge Fund and the North Glasgow Social Inclusion Partnership
- Shared Road plans to create a toolkit for setting up like-minded projects and will launch another project in the Govanhill area of Glasgow in 2006

Contact

Ken Imrie
Project Director
The Prince's Trust
Head Office, 1st Floor, The Guildhall
57 Queen Street
Glasgow G1 3EN
Tel: 0141 204 4409
E-mail: kenneth.imrie@princes-trust.org.uk
Website: www.princes-trust.org.uk

Quotes

'In the early days, local youths stood at one end of the hall, asylum seekers at the other. The taster activities got them together.'

'It's important that the staff team challenge any hostility or racist remarks. The main ethos is respect for each other and good behaviour.'
Ken Imrie

PERSONAL DEVELOPMENT

21 Skye and Falinge Girls' Group, Greater Manchester Police

The Project
The project set up a girls' group in order to bring together girls from one of the local council estates with girls of a similar age (12–16) from local asylum-seeking and refugee communities.

Background
Falinge in Rochdale, Greater Manchester, is an asylum dispersal area into which asylum seekers started arriving in significant numbers about two years ago. Initially young Iraqi men were dispersed to the area and there was community tension and territorial issues. The National Asylum Support Service was subsequently asked to send families. Falinge is a poor estate which prior to the arrival of refugees and asylum seekers experienced a high turnover of tenants.

Why do it?
Although some of the local girls and some of the refugee and asylum-seeking girls went to the same secondary school, they were wary and had little understanding of each other. It was thought that the refugee and asylum-seeking girls were not as involved in local activities as they could be. There was some evidence that they were being bullied. It was felt that boys in the area tended to mix through football but that girls had less opportunity to interact.

Key Concerns
Locals
Primarily they felt that asylum seekers receive preferential treatment and better access to services.

Newcomers
In relation to the project itself, it was sometimes difficult to convince the parents of the girls involved that their daughters would be safe.

Approach and Activities
Team building, trips out and issue-based discussions on topics such as racism and bullying were key activities. Others included self defence, rock climbing and dance/music/drama.

Initially, the girls drew up their own rules such as 'no swearing' and 'no racism'. From then on, the main approach was to let the girls have fun, but there was some direct intervention from the organisers to initiate discussion on racism, bullying and stereotyping. Overall the project was led in a way that was intended to minimise a division of 'the staff' from 'the girls'.

The project drew girls from two nearby council estates: Falinge, where refugee and asylum seekers are dispersed to, and Skye. The two estates are about ten minutes apart. There are territory issues between them, but there were no specific problems known between the two groups of girls. A neutral location, near both estates, was found for the group to meet.

Aims
- To enable the girls to work together and better understand each other's views
- To create a fun and relaxed atmosphere where all the participants felt comfortable

Achievements

- The participants understood that they had things in common with members of the other group
- Forging of new friendships
- Increased confidence amongst the participants
- Dispelled some media 'myths'
- Encouraged the refugee and asylum seeker participants to get involved in other projects

How do we know?
The participants kept diaries and completed feedback forms.

What Made a Difference?

Internal factors

- The host group was carefully chosen to involve girls who would embrace the project as it was important that the initial scheme was a success
- The atmosphere was relaxed, so none of the participants felt under pressure
- Activities such as team building put an emphasis on what brought the girls together
- Having some background knowledge about the refugee and asylum-seeker participants helped the staff know where there might be sensitivities

External factors
Local media reporting in the area has generally been positive toward asylum seekers and refugees.

Key Messages

- Creating a relaxed environment allowed participants to interact comfortably, naturally and under no pressure
- Involving the participants in the organising and managing of the group gave them all confidence and allowed them to forge close relationships with each other

Facts and Figures

- The project was run by an asylum and refugee liaison officer from Greater Manchester Police and funded by Rochdale Federation of Tenants and Residents Association (ROFTRA)
- The first project ran for 11 weeks, with eight host community girls and four from refugee and asylum-seeker backgrounds
- A second group is now running and a third group is starting soon

Contact

PC Tracey Lowe
Community Affairs Department
Rochdale Police Station
The Holme
Rochdale OL16 1AG
Tel: 0161 856 8452
E-mail: Tracey.Lowe@gmp.police.uk

Quotes

'It was cool! Great session (about team building and problem solving). All of us felt valued and able to question and say what we didn't understand…we worked together solving problems, discussing and reasoning. We are more aware now of the needs of others in our group and our self confidence has improved.'
Extract from participant's diary

Summary

There is an interesting diversity in the types of projects detailed in this Handbook. However, there is also a common thread that links these initiatives. Namely, the identification of the positive effects that contact with refugees and asylum seekers and the provision of information about this group can have on community relations.

Some projects employed these in a fairly passive way, for example the Victoria Estate Action Group which saw value in an informal drop-in centre. Others are more proactive, such as Refugee Action's Refugee Awareness Project, which presents 'myth-busting' information to meetings of local residents groups and recruits volunteers from both communities to make presentations.

The types of activities chosen by projects were varied in nature – from work shadowing and cooking to house renovation and football – but represented common approaches to bridge-building. In relation to 'contact theory', getting people together to share an activity, over and above simply being in the same place at the same time, was perceived as the main strategy most likely to succeed. However, the end result of the joint activity is also seen as significant by project leaders. The Refugee Accommodate Project in Beeston Hill brings people together not as an end in itself but for the wider goal of regenerating the local neighbourhood for everyone. The Derwent Zambezi Association organised a social event in the local pub with the express intent of people getting to know each other.

Information activities include producing fact sheets, building relationships with local press and holding public meetings. The common approach that links these is one of raising awareness amongst individuals or agencies by presenting facts about the true experiences and situation of refugees and asylum seekers. This ranges from the strategic approach of the Regional Community Cohesion Project, which shares information about racist crime with local authorities and crime and safety agencies, to the individual approach of the Refugee Awareness Project which personalises information through refugee speakers at local residents meetings.

The case studies have shown that the effectiveness of these strategies is determined both by context-specific circumstances and project-specific factors. In terms of context, geography, socio-economic conditions, demographics, politics and media shaped the projects and their outcomes. Participants in the Derwent Refugee Community Development Support Project felt that the small numbers of refugees and asylum seekers in an otherwise predominantly white and well-established community made it easier for the project to target and focus its work. Shared Road in Glasgow pointed out that the Scottish Executive's express welcoming of new immigration, backed by an increasingly positive local and national press, was conducive to community relations work. Conversely, in interviews a good number of projects felt that 'get tough' UK immigration policies presented external challenges to their work, and they regarded them as a hindrance, while national media coverage focusing on illegalities in the asylum system often negated the more positive stories about asylum seekers that they were trying to put across. With a good number of initiatives based in areas with complex social problems, many project leaders talked of the importance of accommodating fear of crime and harassment as a starting point for engagement.

Commonly mentioned project-specific factors included partnerships, leadership, commitment, time, and learning by doing. Every project interviewed said that it could not have achieved what it had done alone. The more active the partners, the better the outcome. When this incorporated larger institutional support, the effectiveness of the work was significant enhanced. The successful engagement of young people in the Shared Road project was largely due to its promotion by the local secondary school and police reassurance of parents.

The hard work and commitment of influential individuals is another common factor. Councillors who put party politics aside were key to the success of the work of the Camden and Enfield Scrutiny Commissions.

Most project leaders reported that change takes time. 'We have only just started; this is an ongoing process,' was a commonly held view. Lastly, in some cases projects were evolving, learning by mistakes and changing their practice accordingly. Interviewees told us that reflection and 'learning by doing' are essential components that inevitably mirror the evolving dynamics of communities as they learn to adjust to one another.

In gathering this information it also became clear that a number of other constraints impeded the success of projects. Funding was mentioned by almost everyone interviewed as a major constraint. It was not necessarily the amount that concerned people, although that was undoubtedly important, but more the uncertainty of securing ongoing funding. Building bridges between communities is a long-term commitment and the challenge of sustainability is ever present.

Lack of resources also impacted on evaluation. When researchers asked projects how they knew they had created friendships, reduced community tensions or changed attitudes, smaller projects relied on anecdotes, informal feedback and personal observation. Larger ones had developed a variety of tools that measured the attitudes of one group only, usually asylum seekers and refugees. A lack of systematic evidence gathering and analysis not only impacts on small projects which need to prove their effectiveness to funders, but also on wider learning implications for the field of community relations research, policy and practice.

It was clear from many of the projects that formally measuring impact was problematic. More broadly, evaluations of these types of initiatives to date have not been systematic or particularly focused on assessing impact. This may be due to the fact that measuring the success of initiatives designed to influence attitudes and inter-group dynamics is methodologically and ideologically challenging. How is success defined and how do you measure it? There are no agreed criteria for measuring opinion change or the wider processes of building 'good' community relations. Some projects, such as the Refugee Awareness Project, are contributing towards thinking in this area by interviewing not only the participants in the meetings they organise but others who are not directly involved in the process. There remains a question mark, however, over how very small initiatives might feasibly be able to contribute to wider thinking.

Most projects are not measuring impact outside the confines of their own work. One commonly held view is that the 'wider community' was not being reached and that many projects 'preach to the converted'. This is unsurprising given the local nature and scale of some initiatives but raises questions about the acceptance of new communities at a broader level. Nevertheless, the majority of projects reported positive changes in wider community dynamics. Common views were that '[local] people are getting used to them', 'refugees are feeling more comfortable now' or 'things have improved since hitting a low point [such as a violent assault on an asylum seeker]'. A number of project leaders said that in their experience, while mistrust and racism remain, community relations showed more signs of improvement than of deterioration.

Despite an extensive call for projects, the research team came across very few led by refugees. This may partly be explained by the fact that many Refugee Community Organisations (RCOs) are involved in the process of forming 'bonds' within their own community before reaching out to form 'bridges' with other groups. It is also likely that RCOs, which are typically run by one or two volunteers on a minimal or non-existent budget, would not have the capacity to take part in the research. It raises wider questions about the lack of participation of refugees in politics whether at the local or national level. There is an urgent need to research this issue further.

Furthermore, as it was outside the scope of this research to include the perspectives of project beneficiaries, it has not been possible to include the views of refugees and asylum seekers themselves, or of established residents. According to the majority of project leaders spoken to, one of the main concerns of newcomers was safety and security, indicating that the first priority of asylum seekers and refugees is finding a safe space where they can establish themselves. The chair of the majority refugee-led Derwent Zambezi Association felt that it is only later in the settlement process that newcomers feel ready to engage more with the local community, suggesting the importance of allowing relationships to develop naturally from an initial position of security.

On the other hand, the concerns of established residents most commonly centred on competition for already stretched local resources and the perception that newcomers were taking more than their fair share. This indicates that initiatives that address both sets of concerns are likely to have most impact for both groups. The Greater Pollock Settlement and Integration Network felt that its Community Café not only provides a welcoming space for new residents but that its cost price fresh fruit 'barra' also offers a new resource for the benefit of everyone.

The media was identified by all project representatives as potentially playing a constructive or destructive role in bridge-building initiatives. Most believed that hostile national media coverage of asylum issues was a key factor in shaping the concerns of established residents. On the other hand, the local media was viewed as a potential ally for building positive relations. Significantly, almost every interviewee noted a change in the attitude of the local media over the last five years, from a position of hostility to a growing interest in positive human interest stories, such as the achievements of a refugee football team or an ongoing anti-deportation campaign. Many felt that engaging with the local media was important for getting the message across. However, others had preferred to ignore the media, usually through reasons of caution or lack of capacity.

It is clear from these initiatives that while there are common approaches, their success or otherwise is shaped by both internal project design and dynamics and wider contextual factors. The practitioners who were interviewed identified the following key lessons from their work:

- physical proximity does not guarantee good relations. Engagement in shared activities with a common goal is likely to be more effective;
- the personalisation of information, such as using refugee speakers at schools, is an effective way of influencing perceptions;

- personal relationships have the most potential for changing attitudes;
- relationships should not be forced, but allowed to develop naturally;
- newcomers need a safe and secure space before bridging can begin effectively;
- the concerns of established residents and newcomers are different. Generally, for one side they relate to competition for resources, for the other to safety and security. Both need to be taken into account;
- the integration of newcomers is a two-way exchange. Each side must adapt to the other and change accordingly;
- reflection and learning must be part of the process;
- engaging the local media, which is more likely than the national media to be positive about asylum seekers and refugees, should be considered;
- partnership working is essential;
- involving local institutions and public figures contributes to wider acceptance and sustainability;
- building bridges is a long process. This needs to be recognised by funders.

Concluding Remarks

In preparing this Handbook and interviewing project staff it became clear that across the UK people recognised a need for community-led initiatives that addressed an issue of local concern, namely, the need to forge links across groups in society. There is considerable entrepreneurial spirit and energy, and a genuine desire to accommodate new arrivals even where there is hostility and a gulf in understanding. In general, the projects made real progress in encouraging contact between formerly isolated groups, and also in improving the knowledge that different groups had of each other.

There is an opportunity to build on this momentum and to provide targeted support to enable positive lessons to be replicated elsewhere in the country and existing projects to be sustainable in the long term. The issue of funding was recognised by all projects as critical to success. Funding was available from a wide range of sources including central and local government and the voluntary sector. However it tended to be short-term (mainly on a 12-month project cycle), its accounting procedures can be onerous for smaller organisations, and, in some cases, the institutional priorities and restrictions that come with it can impede creative thinking.

The research has shown that formal and independent evaluations are rarely undertaken and this means it is difficult to verify impact and to understand what works and why. Evaluations are important in ensuring that consultation is an integral part of the project from its inception, in part because this guarantees that the views and concerns of stakeholders are taken into account. Where refugees are typically excluded from local political processes, this kind of consultation can play an essential role in promoting participation. There is a need to develop and make available a systematic and appropriate evaluation framework that can identify and promote standards for measuring the impact of initiatives in the following key areas: quality and density of contact, social capital, the provision and impact of information, and community safety and well-being.

Bibliography

R. Bach, *et al.*, *Changing Relations: Newcomers and established residents in US communities* (New York, Ford Foundation, 1993).

A. Clark, *The Reporting and Recording of Racist Incidents Against Asylum Seekers in the North East of England* (Newcastle, University of Northumbria, 2004).

G. Craig, A. Dawson, S. Hutton, N. Roberts and M. Wilkinson, *Local Impacts of International Migration: The information base* (Hull, University of Hull, 2004).

L. D'Onofrio and K. Munk, *Understanding the Stranger: Final report* (London, ICAR, 2004).

ECRE, *Good Practice Guide on the Integration of Refugees in the European Union* (Athens, Greek Council for Refugees, 2004).

N. Finney, *Asylum Seeker Dispersal: Public attitudes and press portrayals around the UK* (University of Wales Swansea, PhD thesis, 2004).

N. Finney and E. Peach, *Attitudes Towards Asylum Seekers, Refugees and Other Immigrants: A literature review for the Commission for Racial Equality* (London, CRE, 2004).

H. Gould, *A Sense of Belonging* (London, Creative Exchange, 2005).

R.L. Hewitt, *Asylum Seeker Dispersal and Community Relations: An analysis of development strategies* (London, Goldsmith's College, University of London, 2002).

M. Hollands, 'Upon Closer Acquaintance: The impact of direct contact with refugees on Dutch hosts', *Journal of Refugee Studies* 14(3), 2001, pp. 295–314.

ICAR, *Media Image, Community Impact: Assessing the impact of media and political images of refugees and asylum seekers on community relations in London. Report of a pilot research study* (London, ICAR, 2004).

G. Lemos, *The Search for Tolerance: Challenging and changing racist attitudes and behaviour among young people* (London, Joseph Rowntree Foundation, 2005).

M. Lewis, *Asylum: Understanding public attitudes* (London, IPPR, 2005).

H. Meert, K. Peleman and K. Stuyck, 'The Establishment of Asylum Centres: Creating a social basis for a dignified asylum policy', paper presented at the Annual Conference of the Royal Geographical Society (with the Institute of British Geographers), London, September 2003.

A. Rudiger, 'Integration of New Migrants: Community relations' in S. Spencer, ed., *New Migrants and Refugees: Review of evidence on good practice* (Oxford, Oxford University Press, Forthcoming).

G. Valentine and I. McDonald, *Understanding Prejudice: Attitudes towards minorities* (London, Stonewall, 2004).

K. Wren, *Building Bridges: Local responses to the resettlement of asylum seekers in Glasgow: Scottish Centre for Research on Social Justice, Report No. 1* (Glasgow, SCRSJ, 2004).

ICAR

The Information Centre about Asylum and Refugees (ICAR) is an academic research and information organisation based at City University. ICAR aims to raise the level of public debate and understanding of asylum in the UK context and to encourage evidence-based policymaking. Established in March 2001, ICAR collects, collates, analyses and disseminates information, research findings, statistics and other data about issues related to asylum and refugees. Through a range of web-based products, project work, commissioned research and participation in conferences, workshops and training sessions, ICAR makes this information and analysis widely available to researchers, service providers, the media, policymakers, refugee populations and members of the general public. ICAR's work concentrates on improving understanding of the asylum system and developing the understanding of the refugee populations that are resident in the UK. While primarily focused on the UK, ICAR also recognises the importance of the global forced migration context, particularly in relation to the internationalisation of asylum policy and the complexities of cross-border population movements.

ICAR
School of Social Sciences
Northampton Square
London
EC1V 0HB

Tel: 020 7040 4596
E-mail: icar@city.ac.uk
Website: www.icar.org.uk

Calouste Gulbenkian Foundation

The Calouste Gulbenkian Foundation is based in Lisbon, with a Portuguese Cultural Centre in Paris, and a grant-giving Branch in London for the United Kingdom and the Republic of Ireland. The United Kingdom Branch has a reputation for recognising and initiating innovative ideas and for the past fifty years has been a pioneering funder of developments in contemporary arts, education and social policy, as well as promoting Portuguese culture. It also regularly commissions and publishes books and reports which reflect and promote its current priorities, concerns and areas of interest.